EMPLOYEES NOT DOING
WHAT YOU EXPECT

- ➢ **Find out why**
- ➢ **Fix it**
- ➢ **Prevent it in future**
- ➢ **Turn negative situations into positive relationships**

By Greg Schinkel and Irwin Schinkel

EMPLOYEES NOT DOING WHAT YOU EXPECT

By

© GREG SCHINKEL AND IRWIN SCHINKEL 2005

Published by:
Unique Development Corporation
45 Meg Drive
London, Ontario, Canada
N6E 2V2
orders@uniquedevelopment.com
http://www.uniquedevelopment.com

Unattributed quotations are by Greg Schinkel and Irwin Schinkel.

ISBN printed.   0-9734-2530-X
ISBN PDF ed.   0-9734-2530-1
ISBN Practical Application Guide 0-9734-2530-2

First Printing 2005
Printed in Canada

COPYRIGHT

National Library of Canada Cataloguing in Publication

Schinkel, Greg, 1967-
    Employees not doing what you expect: find out why, fix it, prevent it in future, turn negative situations into positive relationships / Greg Schinkel and Irwin Schinkel. – 1st ed.

Includes index.
ISBN 0-9734253-0-X

    1. Problem employees. 2. Organizational effectiveness. 3. Employee motivation. I. Schinkel, Irwin, 1932- II. Title.

HF5549.S24 2005 658.3'045 C2003-906824-2

THIS BOOK IS DEDICATED TO

God, who is the source of our natural abilities.
The Lord, our leader by example.
The Spirit that moves us to be caring and competent leaders.

~

Our clients, who have so willingly shared their most challenging experiences.

~

Our families, who have encouraged and supported us.

~

You, our readers, who we expect will benefit from these experiences and insights.

Contents

Contents

Getting Started

Situations and secrets

In workshops and consulting situations, leaders tell us their stories of sleepless nights, gut-wrenching confrontations and workplace negativity. They confide how it wears them down, tears at their confidence and undermines their desire to continue.

Others say it's a never ending series of petty complaints, lack of cooperation and marginal performance. They feel worn out, stressed and frustrated. They see no light at the end of the tunnel and no end to the pressure and pain.

Having worked with thousands of leaders from lead hands to executives, in organizations large and small, we've learned that their experiences are much the same. People hassles and headaches are their most common complaint.

But over the years we've discovered an interesting fact. Not *every* leader experiences these horrific challenges. At training sessions, in conference rooms and at executive retreats there are some who sit quietly, saying little. They don't brag. They don't complain. They're not smug or self-satisfied. It's just that they have two secrets. First, they've learned how to correct people problems in a way that minimizes recurrence. Second, they know how to turn negative confrontations into positive relationships.

Using this knowledge they have eliminated most of their problems. They make leadership seem simple and easy. Some are so adept at doing this, that they can be transferred to any department, any location, any organization and within a few months they turn snarling tigers into purring pussycats.

This book will give you the information and the self-confidence to do the same. While some managers develop this ability over many years of trial and error, you can learn the secret from their experiences. You don't have to suffer through the painful difficulties and struggles they had to endure and overcome.

A quick and easy format

To make the learning process as easy as possible, this book has been organized and designed in a specific way.

First, the hundreds of reasons people don't do what we expect have been distilled into the twelve most common reasons, one in each chapter. This makes the information easier to access, use and remember.

Second, the chapters are progressive. The earlier chapters cover situations that occur most often and are easiest to correct. The next few chapters deal with reasons that occur less frequently and are more difficult to change. The final chapters are devoted to those factors that you are less likely to experience but which are serious, difficult to manage and often require professional assistance to solve. This design gives you the information you need in a sequence that lets you solve the most frequent challenges more quickly and easily.

Next, each chapter has a specific structure. In each, we ask "Why?" to identify not only the obvious reason for the problem but the underlying causes. Then a step-by-step linkage from attitudes to results is outlined. This is followed by several true-to-life stories (names and other information have been changed to ensure confidentiality). In each case, we learn exactly what the leader did, the phrases that he or she used most effectively and the way they approached these problems. The stories go further to show how these leaders manage to avoid most of the problems other leaders wrestle with every day, how these leaders treat negative situations as opportunities and correct them in a way that develops and strengthens the employee relationship.

Each chapter ends with observations and quotations to deepen your understanding and inspire you. Finally, there are touches of humor to make your reading more enjoyable.

Three priceless tools

Included in this section are three powerful, multi-purpose tools that you will find useful in any people-oriented situation. The first is the Performance Process diagram which clearly outlines the linkage from attitudes to results. Second, is the Probing for Cause process complete with an example to make it easier to understand and use. Third, there is a short paragraph which explains a more effective and factual way to describe people problems.

1. Understanding the Performance Process

It's important for leaders to consider the factors in the employee's thinking process that affect performance in the workplace. People bring a host of experiences and predetermined opinions to a task. These ideas shape emotional responses that occur almost by reflex. Emotions in turn influence the actions that produce the results that you as a manager seek to change.

The chart below illustrates how attitudes and results are linked:

Performance Process

```
                ┌────────►  Attitudes
                │              │
   E            │              ▼
   x            │           Emotions
   p            │              │
   e            │              │
   r            │              ▼
   i            │            Actions
   e            │              │
   n            │              │
   c            ▲              ▼
   e            │            Results
   s            └──────────
```

Tangible and Intangible

Attitudes are our beliefs, perceptions, viewpoints, and mindset. They are what we *think*, our interpretation of what we see, hear and experience. Attitudes are habits of thinking. They are held in relation to things which may include certain tasks, the boss or fellow employees. They are determined by our beliefs about others, ourselves and the world around us. In fact they influence everything we do. Change an attitude, a belief, and you change the reactions and results.

Emotions are *feelings* that color our actions. These range from love to hate, fear to confidence, attraction to repulsion, and joy to despair. They include envy, jealousy, disgust and dozens of others. However, behavioral psychologists tell us that the two emotions that generally motivate us are our fears and our desires. The fear of losing something we value or the desire to gain something important to us. The "something we value" may be tangible, such as money, home, travel and so on. Or it may be something intangible, such as security, attention, approval, respect, status or a sense of achievement.

Rational thinking can override our emotions and lead us to logical decisions rather than reacting to fleeting moods and emotions. At other times emotions are so strong they take over and short circuit logical thinking.

Actions are behaviors. They include everything we say and everything we don't say, the things we do and the things we don't do, what we pursue and what we avoid. Actions are observable and measurable. They are influenced by our attitudes and emotions. They may be well-planned or impulsive, proactive or reactive. Over time, our actions tend to become habits; we do certain things in certain ways and we do it automatically. Habits save time, but they can be difficult to change and therefore they tend to maintain the current practice.

Results are what is achieved, accomplished, or generated. They are the outcomes, the output, the product of the actions taken. These results may be tangible and expressed in terms of quantity, quality and timeliness, in terms of frequency or duration, or in terms of goals achieved and goals not achieved. There are also intangible results which include co-operation or conflict, resistance or support, satisfaction or dissatisfaction. Because these intangible results are important, methods of measuring them, using interviews, questionnaires and surveys, have been developed and are now used more often.

Attitudes determine our emotions which influence our choice of actions in any situation. These in turn determine the results we achieve which may be what we had in mind and hoped for or may be just the opposite of what we expected.

When a leader understands this linkage he or she is in a strong position to change an unsatisfactory result for the better. Leader and employee both reap the benefits and hopefully the experience leads to a change of attitude that will help prevent the situation from recurring in the future.

2. Probing for Cause and Preventing Problems

Solving people problems is more effective when we follow a process and clearly understand the problem before taking action. Inappropriate action can make the situation worse.

Describing an employee problem in terms of behavior or results is an important first step in correcting the situation. The next step is to determine *why* they are not doing what we expect, not only the most obvious cause, but also the actual, deeper, root cause. The probing process outlined below can be useful.

Let's begin with an example. We have deliberately chosen a simple situation to make these points. First, because it's faster and easier and, second, because it also illustrates how even a minor situation can be irritating if it continues.

For this exercise we are using a **result** type of problem and show it as such:

	Directions	Example
1.	Type of Problem Identify the type of problem (is it a result deficiency or a behavior?)	Result deficiency.
2.	Problem Statement Write a problem statement of one or two lines.	Reports generated by a clerical person are not in the format I expect.
3.	Circumstances Briefly list some of the key facts regarding the circumstances (the person, past performance etc.).	A new person in this position, no previous problems. This may seem minor but it irritates me.
4.	Most Likely Causes Review the 12 reasons people don't do what we expect and select the two or three you think are the most likely causes in this case.	Person doesn't know what I expect. Person thinks what they are doing is acceptable. Person doesn't know how to do what I expect.
5.	Determine the Actual Cause Approach the person in a friendly manner. Mention something positive about the result achieved. Review your expectation. Ask if	*"Good morning Martin. Thanks for the report you left on my desk. It seems correct and complete. However, I do prefer a different format. Have*

	the person needs any information or instruction.	*I mentioned the format I prefer? (Answer is "No"). Would it help if I showed you what I mean?"*
6.	Actual Cause From the person's answer you now know the actual cause.	It was the fact that I hadn't explained what format I preferred and expected.
7.	Corrective Action Take the necessary action to correct the deficiency.	Simply explained the format preferred and the reason. I made sure he knew how and could do it.

This is usually the point at which we say to ourselves, "problem identified, problem solved, task completed." But before we strain an arm patting ourselves on the back, we should ask a few questions. Since this is just an example and we *do* want to get the most out of this book, let's ask several more questions and consider the possible answers:

Q: Why didn't the employee know what I expected?
A: Because I didn't explain what I wanted and why.
Q: Why didn't I explain?
A: Because I was too busy or assumed someone else would, or I didn't think it was that important.

Selecting just one of these possibilities, probe a little further:

Q: Why am I too busy to effectively inform and instruct a new employee?
A: Because I had other tasks and responsibilities I considered more important.
A: Because I am impatient with employees and feel they should know what I expect.
A: Because I don't have time for such trivial tasks.
A: Because I'm so overloaded with work there is no time to show people how to do it right the first time.
A: Because if I don't do it myself it won't be done right.

Asking ourselves "Why?" several times may make us feel uncomfortable but this tension indicates that we are drawing closer to the root cause. We begin to uncover systemic problems and/or management actions or attitudes that need to be changed. Taking action to solve the deeper root cause of problems leads to truly effective problem *prevention*. It results in a more effective organization and in more harmonious relationships with our people.

3.   Describe the Behaviors and Results – Not the Attitudes

Too often, managers describe an employee problem by saying the employee has an "attitude" problem or that the employee has a "negative attitude." These are assumptions which may or may not be correct. Negative attitudes may not necessarily result in unsatisfactory performance. If the employee's negative attitude creates negative behavior, then of course, that is a performance problem. Most people can control or suppress some of the attitudes they have for some period of time but eventually it affects their behaviors and the results they achieve. The difficulty is that no one can observe, touch, or measure attitude. If we say, "You have a bad attitude," to an employee it can lead to a long and acrimonious argument that cannot be settled on the basis of facts. **It is more factual, accurate, and useful to describe an employee problem in terms of observable behaviors or measurable results.**

At this point it is equally important to check your own attitudes and impulses. If you think the employee is careless or lazy, your actions will tend to be negative, your tone of voice, word usage and expression will all convey a negative outlook. You will usually gain a more positive response from the employee if you begin by thinking, "this person likely wants to perform well, how can I best coach him?"

Now you are ready to start Chapter One. As you move forward into each chapter you'll feel the excitement as you recognize your own experiences in the situations we examine. You'll feel your confidence grow as you discover the tools you need to help you as a leader When you finish you'll have experienced the "aha" factor, that "now I understand" feeling and the "so that's the secret" element of discovery.

> *"Often it's what we learn after we think we know it all that is most meaningful, significant, and enduring."*
>
> **– The Authors**

Because

1

They Don't Know
What You Expect

Why?

Because

➤ The employee is new to his or her department or has taken on new responsibilities.

➤ You have just been assigned as manager and the employees are uncertain about your expectations.

➤ A wave of change (new technology, new customers, changed executive goals, corporate restructuring or acquisitions) has created uncertainty among the employees.

In today's ever-changing environment, and with the rapid pace of change, it's easy to find yourself in a situation where neither you nor your employees are clear as to what your expectations of them should be. Confusion and disappointment are the result.

The Linkage: From attitudes to results

When they experience a change in jobs, tasks, duties, or managers, employees believe that someone will tell them what is expected and why it's important. While some take the attitude that change is an opportunity, others may see it as cause for concern.

On an emotional level, they want to do well and would like to be reassured that they will be able to do what is required. At the same time they feel nervous, apprehensive, and unsure of what the manager expects. They're concerned because they don't want to make a mistake or miss something important. Some fear possible criticism or job loss. The better they understand the expectations, the more confident they become. With confidence comes eagerness to prove themselves and their capability.

Some employees take action (or avoid taking action and making decisions) because they feel it is prudent behavior to "play it safe" until they get a "feel" for the situation.

Others who are overzealous and overconfident may tackle tasks without truly understanding the requirements.

The results are that some employees are not doing what you expect. There may be errors and delays as some are not performing efficiently and effectively.

As the following example indicates, the first step is for managers to clearly define a standard of performance.

THE MASTERS WINNERS

Tiger Woods and Mike Weir are both great golfers and have both won the Masters Championship at the Augusta National Golf Club. Therefore we know they can win (they've done it before). However, neither plays a flawless round of golf. They do their best but even their best varies from day to day and course to course.

We could expect them to win every time but that would be unrealistic and unreasonable. So tournament organizers set an expectation level that all players have to meet to be allowed to compete. It's called "the cut." Those scoring higher than "the cut" are eliminated; those scoring lower are allowed into the final rounds. Most professionals set their goals to finish in the top 10 or with a score that is their personal best. Only a few expect to win first place every time.

Similarly, every manager has to develop a personal understanding of what expectations are realistic and achievable. The manager must have a "norm" in mind and realize that, at times, individuals will exceed that norm and on occasion may fall below. With an achievable norm clearly established in his or her own mind, the manager can turn to the question of how best to communicate those expectations to the employees.

PROMISES DON'T PAY THE LOAN

Walter Baxter was the branch manager for a consumer finance company. He hired several new collectors each year. This was a high turnover position, due to the stressful nature of a collector's responsibility. Because Walter hired and trained these people regularly, he had developed an effective startup process. He began by telling the new recruit their duties, the situation, and his expectations.

"Your job," he'd say, "is to personally visit the homes of customers who have not made their payments on time. They've already been reminded with several notices, letters and phone calls. On more than one occasion, they have promised to pay but they haven't kept their promises."

Walter would then tell the new collector that his job was to visit these people and persuade them to do one of three things:

1. Give the collector at least one payment.
2. Accompany the collector back to the office to meet with Walter.
3. Talk to Walter on the telephone in the collector's presence.

"Is that clear?" Walter asked the new collector. "What questions do you have?"

Usually there weren't any questions because he had been specific.

"One thing you *do not do*," he'd conclude with emphasis in order to be absolutely clear, "is to accept another promise of payment. Those are the results I expect, but there are a couple of other items you need to understand. You must never touch the person or threaten them with physical harm. Always control your temper and frustration. Finally, act and dress like a professional to gain the person's respect."

Walter never told the new collector *how* to persuade the customer to pay. The next day he would accompany the new collector on his rounds. After that initial day, Walter would meet with his new employee at the end of each day in his office. He reviewed what the collector had achieved and how they had approached the challenge. He did this by having the collector explain what they had done and why, and the result achieved.

Walter didn't tell the collector this but he knew it was normal for new collectors to accept promises in spite of being told not to do so. Each day Walter restated the three acceptable options and reminded the collector not to accept promises. At this point, Walter had clearly explained his expectations and moved on to point out his indicators of performance. Walter took the customer payment cards and put them conspicuously on the top right corner of his desk.

"If the customer comes in and makes a payment as promised," he said pointedly, "this card won't be on this pile when we meet on Friday. These cards are the indicator of how well you're doing. It's the way we measure your success rate."

Usually, day-by-day, the pile of cards grew instead of declining. The collector watched with dread as they piled up. By Friday of the first week, Walter knew in measurable terms the new employee's natural success rate. He knew something about how he or she thought and how assertive and persuasive they were. The collector knew that Walter was firm in his expectations.

There were no escape hatches. There was no wiggle room, no compromise.

In a friendly way, Walter also set out to change the collector's beliefs and perceptions about borrowers and their behaviors.

"When collectors start with us," he'd say, "they almost always think that all customers are basically honest, want to pay and will pay, if just given a chance. Now it's Friday and you see the stack of cards. These people haven't paid. That's why we say there are only three acceptable options."

After mentally preparing the new collector in this way he asked, "Did all of these people have a telephone?"

The answer, of course, was *yes*.

"So, even if they couldn't pay they could have spoken to me on the telephone, isn't that correct?"

The answer, again, was *yes*.

"Now I have to tell you that the basic reason they didn't pay," Walter continued, "is because you didn't insist on it. You let them off the hook."

With that, Walter would say, "You are ready now to hear the secret to your success as a collector. This secret is, don't leave the customer's premises without achieving one of the three options I gave you."

Telling the collectors this changed their viewpoint and influenced their actions and their results. From this point on the collectors either committed themselves to Walter's expectations and achieved the required results or left the business because their personality did not suit the situation.

Walter's process demonstrates the importance of clearly establishing simple, performance-based expectations. He began by providing a description of the **situation** the employee would experience. Then he listed his expectations in terms of required **results**. Along the way, he mentioned any expectations he had in the area of **behaviors** that were **necessary to the job** and behaviours that were **not allowed**. Walter always identified one or more **indicators** of success and he provided **suggestions** to improve the employee's success ratio. Finally, he **outlined a schedule** for regular, ongoing discussions of progress.

It's also important to note one key aspect to Walter's approach: once he spelled out his expectations, he *never* changed them.

FIND A WAY, NOT AN EXCUSE

Diane, the heroine of our next story, provides an example of how the ongoing application of clearly stated, consistently applied expectations pays off in a time of crisis.

Because of family difficulties, Diane began working on the assembly line in an auto parts plant before graduating from school. Her energy, determination and people skills earned her a promotion to first line supervisor within three years, then six years later to superintendent and, finally, to plant manager.

When the authors first met her, she was the only woman who had achieved this status in any of the corporation's 26 North American plants. Her plant of 500 employees was rated in the corporate top three for performance. But her proudest achievement, which she shared with very few, was an occasion when she kept the plant operating during a fierce snowstorm.

About half of the plant employees were able to struggle to work that day but none of the supervisors could get in. She walked the assembly lines, thanking the employees for making the tremendous effort to be there. Then she challenged them to work without supervisors. In every department she asked, "Can we operate without the supervisor and still make today's shipments?"

Without exception the workers answered, "You bet we can."

"I'm here to support you and help wherever possible," Diane said, "but I can't be everywhere, so here's what we have to do. Today I'm going to be a coordinator. I'll walk through each department every 90 minutes and ask what you need. So get started. Keep the quality high and scrap low. Let's make the numbers for today. Think about what you need for at least two hours ahead and I'll do my best to get it to you."

Then magic happened—an awesome blend of effort, pride, fun, challenge and cooperation. It began slowly and grew hour by hour. Was it the result of one, lone, determined woman? Was it the immensity of the challenge? Was it mutual trust, because they knew her and she knew them?

To this day Diane says she can't say exactly what happened or why. At the end of that day she made a final tour of the plant, thanking her employees, telling them they were heroes. They all knew something incredible had happened. They had all been a part of it and they didn't want it to end. At the end of the day, they were reluctant to leave for home.

Diane believes that employee commitment and performance starts with clear expectations, but it's not just what you say, it's also how you say it. It has to be done in a way that communicates a feeling of being in this together. The implication is, "We need you to do this and I will be here to help you be successful."

When she prepares a newly appointed supervisor for the shop floor, Diane follows a regular routine. She starts with a discussion of their past experiences, which have usually been as hourly paid employees in the plant or with a similar firm in the area.

Then she lists her **required results** for the new supervisor, citing three things they have to make sure they and their people achieve each day:

1. Produce the required *volume* as per schedule, because the company is a "just-in-time" supplier and there are severe penalties for missing a customer's delivery window.
2. Meet the *quality standards* to ensure customer satisfaction. Never ship defective parts just to meet the deadlines.
3. Ensure *employee safety* by watching for and correcting unsafe acts and unsafe conditions.

Diane goes on to list the **behaviors** she expects and insists on. "If you foul up and make a mistake," she says, *"tell me first before someone else plays tattletale. That way I can explain and support you."*

She emphasizes honesty as a must. "Never fudge the numbers in your reports. It destroys the usefulness of information in other departments. Accurate information is essential to both solve problems and plan for production."

The same principle applies to communications with those working under your supervision. "Be a straight arrow," Diane urges. "Give honest answers, encourage them, get to know them and don't use sarcasm. Earn the respect and trust of your employees by **never** threatening them." Continuing she says, "this may seem impossible, but do not use profanity. Even though it's prevalent and everyone seems to be doing it, including actors on T.V. sitcoms, you will gain respect by avoiding it."

In order to make the job easier for themselves, Diane encourages her supervisors to walk through their departments 10 minutes before start time each day to ensure that everything is ready for their employees (i.e. that materials and supplies are in place and the equipment is operational). Next, she tells them to establish a routine and communicate expectations to their people.

"Do this by walking through the department again shortly after starting time," she says. "Ask each person if there are any problems or if there's anything they need. Train them to think and plan ahead. Otherwise, they'll be constantly leaving their stations to find you, interrupting you with requests. Very quickly, they'll turn you into a 'go-fer' instead of a supervisor. You'll be run off your feet and you will have lost control."

Diane's third tip for supervisors is to briefly check each operator's output during their walk to ensure a quality product is being produced and not scrap. If they're on an incentive system, they may be tempted to ignore quality to make their targets. "At the same time," she says, "be friendly and watch for potential safety problems."

Fourth, she tells supervisors to make sure there are accurate and up-to-date work instructions at every workstation and that each employee has been trained to do their job correctly. "Take a personal interest in training the employee. If you delegate the actual training to another employee, be certain that the trainer follows an effective process. Personally follow up later in the day and again the next day and ask the new employee to describe what they are doing, how they are doing it and why it's important."

Diane draws on her own experience when she describes how she communicated expectations to new employees. She uses a blank sheet of paper, draws a line across the middle and on the top half she writes, "What You Can Expect of Me," and on the bottom half, "What I Expect of You." Then she writes down these items:

What You Can Expect of Me:

- ➤ To be provided with safety items and safety instructions.
- ➤ To be paid on time every week.
- ➤ To receive an accurate paycheck.
- ➤ That I will listen and help if you're having some difficulty or problem.
- ➤ To be treated with courtesy and respect.

What I Expect of You:

- ➤ That you will properly use the safety items and will work in a safe manner.
- ➤ That you will do your work right the first time and follow posted work instructions.
- ➤ That you will be here on time every day.

> That if you have a health or personal problem you will tell me as soon as you know that it's going to affect your attendance.
> That you will listen and help if I'm having a difficulty or problem.
> That you will treat me and others with courtesy and respect.
> That you will tell me if you cannot meet any of these expectations.

When you review Diane's expectations and her thorough method of communicating them, you realize that what happened on the day of that snowstorm may have been magic, but the magic was no accident.

WE ARE NOT JUNK DEALERS AND PROUD OF IT!

A newly appointed General Manager didn't mince words when talking to his employees for the first time,"You want to know what I expect of us all? It is simply this:

1. We don't accept junk.
2. We don't produce junk.
3. We don't ship junk – never to our customers and never to each other.

"Therefore," he concluded, "we can be proud of what we produce, proud of each other, and proud of ourselves."

Expectations are best when they are brief, to the point and memorable.

When and why does this type of problem occur?

Employees are most likely not to know what you expect of them when they're new to their positions or departments. It can also happen when there are changes in management, in technology, in location, processes, or policies.

The reasons *why* confusion occurs are usually linked to the change of circumstances. A new manager may be uncertain about what the expectations should be. An experienced manager may have trouble setting realistic expectations when there have been significant changes in equipment, materials, processes, people, products or contractual agreements.

Variations of this problem

When employees don't do what you expect, the problem can express itself in a number of different ways. The employees may say they don't know *why* they should do a job a certain way. They may know what to do but not how well and how quickly it should be done. Their lack of understanding might register as *fear* of making a mistake. Performance may be unsatisfactory because the employees feel it's better to wait until they are told what's expected of them. Even if they've been told, they may still hesitate or make errors because they're unsure of how performance will be evaluated, or how well the work must be done.

Fixing it and preventing it in future

When you experience an employee performance problem, be sure the person or people concerned know what you expect and why:

> ➤ In a friendly way ask them if they know what you expect of them. Acknowledge and reinforce those answers that

are correct. Ask them to eliminate those behaviors that are not applicable and to adjust those that need to be changed.

➤ Ask, "Is there anything now that you don't understand?" Confirm by asking, "Can I count on you to meet these expectations from now on?"

➤ Do this at the earliest opportunity for a private discussion once the problem is realized.

Great managers and leaders prevent problems by communicating clear expectations. In some organizations these are in the form of job descriptions developed and provided by the Human Resources Department. Sometimes they are written on the basis of **Results**, sometimes on the basis of **Activities or Functions**, sometimes they are simply a long list of **Tasks**. All of these have some degree of usefulness.

Better yet, go further by describing what you expect in terms of:

➤ **Key Results–** The key elements of the position will usually number three to seven major measurable outputs.

➤ **Indicators–** Identify the indicators you and the individual will use to determine the level of performance.

➤ **Major Activities–**Actions required to achieve the results. What does the person have to do to gain the expected results?

➤ **Tasks–**A list of tasks can be useful in some situations. However, long lists of tasks tend to detract from the Key Results and can result in debates about "who does what."

➤ **Rules of Conduct–** Are guides for employees' personal behavior. Many companies have these printed as a Code of Conduct booklet.

➤ **Reporting**– A description or organizational chart indicating to whom the person reports.
➤ **Dress Codes**– Some organizations now have this area defined because of legal, governmental, contractual or customer requirements, others do not.

Seldom do organizations spell out expectations in all of these areas. This is only done for areas significant to the position and the desired performance. As a manager it's up to you to identify which of the above are required to ensure your performance expectations are being met.

Observations

When changes are occuring in greater numbers and with increased urgency in your organization, there is a need to discuss expectations more frequently.

Develop expectations at a meeting separate from and before a performance review meeting.

Offer helpful suggestions on making the job easier and point out potential pitfalls.

The better trained and more experienced the employee is, the less they need to be told *how* to do the job. Leave it to them unless there is only one correct and acceptable method.

Avoid sabotaging the expectation process by weakening your expected outcomes, ignoring the actual results or skipping the suggestions or follow-up steps.

"What you expect and *inspect* will usually get done."
                                            – Anonymous

A Smile Break

"If you don't expect to succeed the first and every time, skydiving is not for you!"
                                            – Anonymous

Because

2

They Think What They're Doing Is
Acceptable

Why?

Because
No one has commented on or complained about what they are or
are not doing.

"Problem, what problem? Whatever we're doing must be
okay. No one has said otherwise!" Employees do what is
expected – to the degree it is accepted. When no one from
management expresses concern, why should they do more?
Sometimes they are doing what's expected of them, but they
could be doing more. Short cuts creep into work routines and
become short circuits. Often, managers have no idea it's
happening until things get too relaxed, productivity declines and
they realize that things aren't what they should be.

The Linkage: From attitudes to results

Employees believe that the manager in charge will tell
them when they have to "do better, do different, or do more."

They assume that they must be doing enough because no one has complained. A few believe that to do more would be foolish and unrewarding. In some cases doing more could result in complaints from others who don't want to be "shown up."

After awhile in a given position, people find their "comfort zone," and do what they feel is "enough" at an easy pace.

If the manager doesn't communicate any concerns, the only way employees can find out what is acceptable is to *reduce* their effort. If the manager comments after that, they have defined what's acceptable by learning what the *lower* limits of performance are. They identify what behaviors and results usually generate payoffs (in the form of praise and recognition) and what behaviors generate penalties (such as negative comments or more serious warnings). If the manager avoids comment over a prolonged period, performance and productivity will gradually decline.

The results are that as the situation is tolerated, the behaviors become more prevalent and pervasive. Eventually the company finds that not only has productivity declined, but quality has become a problem, deliveries are delayed and in extreme cases the company becomes uncompetitive.

A "FLASH" OF INSIGHT

Keith was a plant manager and, one day during a visit from the authors, he dropped heavily into a chair in Human Resources and said, "I need a coffee, I'm frustrated."

We asked what was bothering him.

"When I walk through the plant," he replied, "I'm seeing something with my eyes and my gut is telling me something is wrong but my brain hasn't decided what it is."

Two days later he was obviously more relaxed. "Well I finally figured it out," he said. "I must have walked through that dog-gone plant a dozen times before it clicked. At last I realized it was the welding flashes."

Keith explained that he had 37 welders on the job, but when he walked through the plant he only saw five or six welding flashes. That meant only 10 or 15 percent of the welders were actually working. When he looked more closely, he saw that the others were standing around or sitting in groups looking at blueprints, specification lists, or just talking.

"How did you handle it?" we asked.

"It was easy," Keith said. "I just went to each group and asked if they had a problem I could help them with. In every case they said, 'No, we've figured it out,' and returned to welding."

Keith took the opportunity when speaking with the welders to tell them they were the best in that part of the country. He pointed out that the contract for the new vehicles they were working on was one of the most important the company had ever had. "The customer needs these units," he told them. "Let's give them the best quality, delivered on time. I know we can do it."

With one simple question to the welders—"Do you have a problem I can help you with?"—Keith corrected the situation. The case is an excellent example of how, by asking him- or herself a simple question (our good friend "Why?"), a manager can probe to the root of a problem.

Most of Keith's welders weren't welding. *Why?* Because it was easier not to, and no one in management had said anything to them that indicated there was a concern. *Why?* Supervisors didn't realize what was happening (and not happening). *Why?* Because they were new to the department and although they had been trained in basic supervision, the safety requirements, and report preparation, they did not know how to determine productivity by observation. *Why?* Management hadn't developed the expectations and indicators for their supervisors. *Why?* Because this was a startup situation with a new product. and they didn't recognize the need.

Keith corrected the situation by scheduling a production meeting with the supervisors and general supervisors, not to "give 'em hell" but to share what he had learned.

He admitted that he, too, had missed what was happening, and then he mentioned the importance of the contract and the need to be attentive to the performance and needs of the employees.

THEY TEED-OFF TO A SELF-REWARD

Sometimes, both individuals and organizations perform to expecations and accomplish preset goals, but they are achieving less than what is actually possible. That is, they are performing below true potential.

Take Ralph who, as a corporate CEO, had a situation similar to Keith's but at the executive level.

Like Keith, Ralph had an uneasy feeling that something was wrong at one of his company's divisions. Profitability had been outstanding but was beginning to show some small declines. Ralph was also troubled by the fact that, on occasion, when he called the General Manager on a Wednesday, the GM was not available. Corporate people returning from visits to that division commented that there seemed to be an absenteeism problem. Believing in the adage "where there's smoke there's fire," Ralph formed a team comprised of the VP Human Resources, VP Manufacturing and VP Finance and scheduled a charter aircraft to take them to the division's location.

They timed it so that they departed at 5:30 a.m. and were at the division by 7:30 a.m. Ralph went directly to the General Manager's office to await the arrival of the GM and his executive assistant. The VP Human Resources was assigned to monitor arrivals at the main entrance to the offices and the VP Manufacturing immediately went to tour the plant.

Within minutes, they had learned that all eight members of the senior management team were away golfing and that this was a normal weekly event. The VP Human Resources checked the arrivals of office employees and found that 29 percent arrived late. Most were less than 30 minutes late but a few were almost an hour late. In the plant, the situation was not as serious but supervisors admitted that tardy arrivals and absenteeism were a growing problem. To the team of visitors it was clear that the problem was greater than golf or tardiness; a general feeling of relaxation, a lack of urgency and diminished effort permeated the division.

When Ralph's team met in the boardroom Ralph summed it up in one sentence, "They've become fat and lazy."

Then he went on to explain the reason. "They have been focused on beating last year's results and the budget instead of maximizing the potential profits and market share available. Our expectations of this division have obviously been too low and because they were beating the budget we haven't been paying attention to the situation here."

Ralph decided that the team would stay and confront the errant golfers when they returned. In the meantime, he asked his VP Finance to meet with key managers in the Finance Department to review performance reports and forecasts and to formulate possible stretch goals (targets that would challenge the division to exceed the "must do" levels of management's expectations). Next, he scheduled a meeting for late afternoon and asked that two groups be advised to attend: first, the golfing executives and, second, those managers who normally reported to them.

It was a large group that convened at 3:30 P.M. in the conference room. There was no banter, no conversation at all, just apprehension, tension and fear.

While preparing for this meeting Ralph had considered many options including terminating the whole senior management team or terminating the General Manager and canceling scheduled salary increases and bonuses for some or all. He was angry and his impulses were to punish these people. Every option he first considered was negative. He had before him the recommendations of his VPs of Finance, Human Resources and Manufacturing and their stretch targets. He was tempted to blast the golfers and do it in front of their subordinates.

Instead, he didn't say a word for over a minute. Quietly, he looked at each person directly and held his or her gaze for seconds that seemed like centuries. Then he slowly said,
"Each of you is an intelligent, capable, and experienced manager. Individually and as a group you have grown this division and made it profitable. At one time or another I have approved your performance reviews, salary increases and bonuses. You have had my trust and respect."

Ralph likened the situation to a black grease stain on a white shirt. It wasn't just the golfing on company time, it was the fact that the bad habit of a few had set a negative example for the employees in general.

"My first inclination was to terminate one or a number of you," he said. "But that would have damaged your careers and injured your families for years to come. I've considered imposing punitive goals that would keep you working day and night."

"I've decided to do neither. I believe that you've learned your lesson and that this will never happen again. Instead I am going to leave you all with an assignment."

He told the managers that his team would return in one week. At that time, he said he expected to be told what staffing changes, what practices, and reporting changes would be made at the division.

"You will tell us what you are committed to achieving." Ralph concluded. "Tell us, then show us, what you are truly capable of accomplishing by working to true potential."
With those words the team left.

Ralph put the onus directly where it belonged, on the divisional executive committee. He could have set the tough new targets but then they would have been *his* goals. This way they would be the *division's* goals (which could have been higher than his). But the ownership of and responsibility for those goals would be theirs alone.

The tangible results of the executive committee's reassessment were: sales revenues up, profits up, staffing levels and costs reduced. The intangible results were: absenteeism reduced, greater teamwork, a tremendous new spirit of achievement and a greater can-do confidence in the workforce.

When and why does this type of problem occur?

Most often people mistakenly think what they're doing is acceptable when we as supervisors and managers focus all of our attention on problems and fail to inspect, praise, support and recognize routine activities that are being performed well. Like the employees, we assume everything is being done according to requirements and fail to monitor, follow up or provide positive feedback.

Carelessness creeps into the workplace because management's attention is elsewhere and there is an assumption that expectations are being met.

Some employees perceive this lack of attention and inspection first as an opportunity to do less or do it poorly.

Variations of this problem

You may hear employees who erroneously think what they're doing is acceptable say things like "I'm doing enough" or "I need to pace myself."

They think they have earned the right to relax, that there's no problem or management would have said something. Some think what they're doing is acceptable because they're just doing "what everyone else is doing."

Why do they think that?

Because they haven't been told anything to the contrary by their manager.

Fixing it and preventing it in future

To become aware of unacceptable behaviours or results in our area of responsibility, we need to:

> Periodically, walk through every part of every operation under our direction (both inside and outside). As we walk, talk and listen, observe employee effort and general conditions.

> Make it a point to inspect some of the final output and examine those areas where rejects, reworks, replacement, and scrap are stored.

> When we recognize negative behaviors or outputs, the most powerful words we can use are, "This is not satisfactory, how quickly can you correct it?" Always follow up on unacceptable situations to ensure they have been corrected promptly.

The way to prevent problems from happening again is to:

> Build opportunities to **see for yourself** what's happening in the plant, office, or field into your timetable.

> **Talk directly** to the employees doing the job. Ask what is going well and what is causing frustrations. Ask the supervisor or manager of the area or department the same questions. Share what you feel is going well and what you are hoping to achieve. Follow up to try to eliminate the causes of their frustrations.

> Be a **"process observer."** Find a vantage point and just stand there for 10 or 15 minutes. Note the level of activity, the pace, the bottlenecks, who is doing what, or doing nothing; the equipment that is operating or not operating; how full the scrap and rework areas are. When you are in the customer service area, ask whether the number of calls is up or down and what customers are saying and asking.

➤ **Recognize, encourage** and **support** what is being done correctly. Be particularly alert to "best ever" achievements and practices and give prompt and enthusiastic praise.

Observations

Too often top management is insulated from reality by layers of supervisors and managers who want to present the best image possible. Therefore they avoid communicating true conditions and circumstances some of which are in desperate need of attention and correction. In other cases, such as Ralph's situation with the golfers, management has expectations that are too low and below potential.

Organizations are often most at risk when their operations are performing well. At these times the tendency is to relax and put forth less effort.

Walk into problems not away from them. They are opportunities for learning, improvement, prevention and significant benefits.

> *"What management tolerates, they propagate."*
> **– Anonymous**

> *"A small leak will sink a great ship."*
> **– Proverb**

> *"In the end, I always believe my eyes rather than anything else."* **– Warren Buffett**

> *"You can observe an awful lot by simply watching."*
> **– Yogi Berra**

A Smile Break

"You are a bureaucrat if you believe more rules will reduce employee problems."   **– Anonymous**

Because

3

They Think That What
They're Doing Is
Not Important

Why?

Because

No one monitors their reports, output, methods, or compliance to standards. There seems to be no interest in whether the work meets requirements and there is no feedback regarding their responsibilities. The policies, procedures, protocols, regulations or standards which they must meet or maintain are virtually ignored by those in authority.

In the era of mass production, multinational corporations and global trade and an increasing proliferation of government regulations, employees often feel that what they are instructed to do is insignificant and unimportant. The same trends cause managers to feel overwhelmed by deadlines, crises and meetings. Therefore monitoring compliance to standards and regulations receives low priority or is ignored totally. Too often, it is viewed as costly, nonessential paperwork or bureaucracy.

Ironically, the very conditions that cause these attitudes come at a time when compliance is more vital than ever.

Consumers shop today in a global village. They may buy locally or on the internet but their purchases come from around the world. Clothing may have been produced in Thailand or India. Electronics may originate in Japan or Malaysia. Food items come from Chile, Mexico or Israel while wine could just as easily come from Australia as it could from California. An automobile which may have been assembled in Canada, the U.S., Germany or Korea, likely has components from a dozen countries.

Consumers have a wider choice than ever before. They insist on variety, style, performance and value. In addition they expect and insist that their purchase be perfect. Good is no longer good enough. It has a flaw? Take it back to the retailer! Price not to their liking? Off they go to the big box store!

The consumer is also better informed and more discriminating. Product problems are quickly exposed in the evening news. Companies must respond promptly with recalls and repairs or replacements.

Injuries and deaths quickly result in class action lawsuits which, in turn, unearth even more complaints, defense and settlement costs are often in the millions and, on occasion, in the billions. The impact on consumer confidence, brand reputation, profitability and investor confidence is immense.

Food production is similarly affected. One cow with purported Mad Cow Disease in Canada quickly impacts the U.S. cattle industry and Japanese consumers, chickens with Avian Flu in China are destroyed by the hundreds of thousands but concerns result in similar actions in other countries.

The travel and hospitality industry was devastated by an outbreak of Severe Acute Respiratory Syndrome (SARS), which began in China and subsequently spread to other countries.

Companies and governments have responded by adopting and enforcing international quality standards, in some cases introducing even more stringent industry regulations and controls.

Our point here is that the effectiveness of these vital measures is dependent on employees and their managers who may not understand or, in some cases, may not care about adherence to these requirements. They do not realize the astronomical impact and costs which can result from ignoring or deviating from certain instructions and procedures.

The Linkage: From attitudes to results

Employees begin to think that the requirements are not absolute, that there is an alternative that is acceptable, or that the requirements are unnecessary, irrelevant or require too much time and effort.

They feel impatient doing something that seems unimportant to anyone in authority or too costly or time consuming. This is particularly true if there is no recognition or feedback from management when they do this routine and repetitive work correctly day after day.

In the absence of attention from management, some individuals begin to take short cuts, to skip some of the steps and to allow a few minor errors. They do this to test the limits. After a few minor errors or "voids" pass without consequence, there is a temptation to further erode performance because it reinforces their belief that compliance is not required and in fact the task is not important at all. Finally, over an extended period of months or even years, the deterioration in effort continues until there may be no effort whatsoever.

The result is that deficiencies and errors occur in output. Since procedures have not been strictly followed, there can be severe repercussions ranging from rejects, returns, to increased scrap rates and customer complains. In extreme cases this may result is injury or death culminating in costly legal settelements.

POISONED BY THEIR WATER

According to the news media, those in the department knew that regular water supply testing was mandated by government regulations. But during two decades there had never been a problem with the water, so testing became what seemed an unnecessary routine. Newspaper accounts indicate no one from the government agency responsible visited the location to check the methods, frequency or the validity of the reports. The person responsible for the testing, confident that the procedures were needless, began to reduce the frequency of actual tests. To insure against the unlikely possibility of a government audit in future, evidently some test results were falsified and filed.

Reporters learned that "faking samples and falsifying records became routine." No one in a position of authority expressed any concern or even interest so, as time went by, the number of actual tests dwindled to nil and the falsified results increased accordingly. Then a torrential downpour washed bacteria from cattle manure from a nearby farm into the shallow town well. The contamination went undetected until the local hospital began to receive patients in Emergency complaining of diarrhea, vomiting and fever. When the Medical Officer of Health became concerned and called the Waterworks Department, he was assured there were no problems with water quality. As the number of patients grew, the Medical Officer of Health called again to discuss the problem and again he was reassured.

Now, finally concerned about the possibility of contamination in the water supply, the waterworks manager restarted testing. Results confirmed that the water was in fact contaminated and the Medical Officer was so advised. He, in turn, informed the waterworks management of the first death attributed to the problem. Fear and frantic effort now ensued. A search began in earnest to find and eliminate the source of the contamination and so prevent additional deaths. At the same time, according to reports, management continued their cover-up.

It would require three more deaths, a total shutdown and cleansing of the whole water system, and a government investigation to pinpoint the cause and to expose the cover-up. The issue reached the courts and the individuals responsible faced a number of criminal charges.

What must have seemed like a small thing to the person doing the tests, evolved into a horrendous loss of life beyond what anyone could have imagined. This "small thing" attitude and a lack of attention and inspection allow a problem such as this to occur.

But a situation in this general category may not even be perceived as a problem. It may simply be seen as part of the normal process, such was the situation in our next example.

A SIMPLE QUESTION OF FORM(S)

It was a large regional replacement parts warehouse, one of several in the corporation's North American network. The equipment, technology and systems were world class and the employees, all 260, were experienced and well trained.

However, a new pair of eyes often sees circumstances differently. Such was the case when Susan was transferred in as warehouse manager. Within days of her arrival she realized that the warehouse's shipping and receiving process was far too slow.

She could have simply called a meeting and told the employees and supervisors to improve it. However, Susan was an astute leader. She realized that it would be much easier and more effective if the people themselves came up with the necessary changes. She decided that a team-based improvement process called Value Analysis (VA) could do what was required. (Value Analysis was developed by a General Electric executive decades ago. It is a team-based method that identifies the purpose of every task or component in a process, then, using brainstorming techniques, finds ways to achieve the required purpose at lower cost.)

At the next employee meeting she told them how much she enjoyed being there and how pleased she was with their performance. Then she talked about how much she had enjoyed being involved with VA teams in other locations. "If some of you would be interested in participating on a team at some time, please let your supervisor know. If there's interest, I'll find an experienced facilitator from head office to lead us, because I don't have the necessary skills."

She added that participation would be totally voluntary and done during company time. Susan got her volunteers. Head office assigned the facilitator she requested, someone who had both the process skills and the people skills to achieve results.

The best opportunity for improvement was soon obvious. A function titled "Prepare Shipping Release" had an elapsed time of four to six days. Questioning revealed that it was a two-page document that authorized the shipment of parts in bulk to a packaging company. The team learned that the actual time required to complete the form was only five to ten minutes. Why then did it take four to six days to get it issued? The employee who regularly prepared the document said it was because she didn't think it was a priority compared to her other duties.

"I wish someone would have *told* me that it was important," she said.

Now that she understood the form's significance she would complete it immediately on receipt. With this simple change, elapsed time was reduced from four-to-six days to an hour or less. Cost to implement was nil. Savings due to reduced turnaround time was in the thousands. Of course the team found other improvements as well.

Susan gave full credit to the team, personally thanking each person with an individual letter. She took them all out for lunch, and arranged for an article in the company's employee newsletter congratulating the team on its efforts.

In this particular case, the process wasn't causing the problem. It was the fact that the person doing the task didn't understand the importance of the task as it related to the overall.

Another way of saying it would be that the employee didn't know how relevant this one task was to the big picture, nor the extent to which "time was money."

ACCUSATION AND FALLOUT

It was early December and automobile dealers were offering unheard of incentives and financing rates. Andy Simpson decided to use this opportunity to trade in his vehicle at the dealership where he had it serviced. From his first inquiries to the final offer, it all went without a hitch. Andy didn't let on, but he couldn't believe how low the monthly payments were for a three-year lease, therefore before signing he visited three other dealers, who sold the same vehicle. In every case they quoted a monthly rate much higher than the offer he already had.

Next day, Andy visited the dealership and signed the offer. It was reviewed by the Business Manager and endorsed by the Sales Manager. The deal was done and delivery scheduled for two weeks later. Andy was elated but he suspected that something was wrong, that the deal was too good to be true

Three days after the deal was signed Andy received a call from the Sales Manager, Tom Elliott. He introduced himself and asked if Andy was happy with the deal on his new car.

"Of course," he answered. "Yes, I'm very happy with the car, the dealership, and with the deal."

"Well, we're not happy," Elliott said bluntly. In a brusque tone of voice he continued, saying, "The car you traded in was a 1997 model and not a 1999 model as you told our salesman. We feel that you deliberately mislead him."

The Sales Manager's accusatory, sneering tone and choice of words were a red flag waved in Andy's face. In the same tone, Andy demanded to know how he could have mislead the salesman, when the salesman had the car registration for reference, when the model year was readable in the front windshield as part of the vehicle's V.I.N. number, and when the car had been serviced at that dealership for the past two years.

"Your appraiser looked at it," Andy added, "the correct model year was on the offer to purchase, your business administrator looked over the offer and you approved the offer."

But Elliott wouldn't accept any responsibility for the fiasco. Instead he raised his voice and continued to accuse Andy of cheating the dealership until Andy finally hung up.

We should enlighten you about Andy. He's the kind of guy who'll bend, but if you start beating him, look out! He knew he had the upper hand and he was determined to see what the dealership would do next. That would tell him if he wanted to continue to deal with this company.

Andy deliberately waited four days to allow time for word of this situation to make its way up to the owner. Then he called Ken Kendall, the President, introduced himself and said, "I guess by now you've heard my name and the problem." Kendall responded that he had heard one side of the story but would very much like to hear Andy's side. When they met next day at the dealership, Ken Kendall thanked Andy for taking the time to come in.

"Mr. Simpson," he said, "we pride ourselves on how we treat customers and obviously something has gone badly wrong here. Please tell me, step by step, what happened."

Andy told him the whole story, including his account of Elliott's telephone call with its obnoxious, accusatory tone.

"Anything else that you can remember and would like to tell me?" Kendall asked.

Andy responded, "As I've gone through this sequence, I think I know where the problem started."

It had suddenly dawned on Andy that, during their first meeting, he had told the salesman that he had purchased the car in 1999. The salesman had written that fact on a yellow, lined notepad. Andy told him that he had purchased the car as a used vehicle but the salesman never did ask the actual model year of the trade-in.

Kendall leaned back, satisfied that he now knew the whole story and the root causes. "Thank you, again, for coming in Mr. Simpson," he said. "Your visit today tells me that my people did follow the proper process but that all four made serious errors. The salesman didn't think it was important to look at the V.I.N. himself, the appraiser didn't think it was important to verify the information the salesman had given him.

To this list of gaffes Kendall added the fact that the business administrator was new in the position and didn't catch the error on the offer to purchase. Then Kendall apologized for the errors as well as the Sales Manager's inexcusable behavior on the telephone.

In the wake of the incident, Kendall spoke with the staff involved, built checks into the sales process and personally monitored how the new administrator was being trained.

Knowing that Andy would receive a Customer Satisfaction Survey from the manufacturer asking how satisfied he was with his dealership experience, Kendall offered a fair settlement. Because he was impressed with Kendall's friendliness, openness and professionalism, Andy agreed.

When and why does this type of problem occur?

People are most inclined to think that expectations are not important when there has been inattention or a lack of follow-up from management.

It happens:

> ➤ When new or transferred people are not instructed in the importance of the procedures, standards etc. or are not advised that they are mandatory.
> ➤ When changes have been introduced in management, materials, supplies or technology and these seem to make the requirements irrelevant.

➤ When audits and inspections are not done.
➤ When people are not held accountable for noncompliance.
➤ When people are angry with the manager or company, or are bored by seemingly unimportant and repetitious work or they're just lazy and avoid the effort.

Most human beings dislike doing anything that they feel is unnecessary or unimportant. They need regular reassurance and positive feedback. It's also true that people generally would rather do things in a way that requires less attention, energy or time.

But in many if not most cases, it's the lack of awareness on the part of management which allows this problem to begin and then grow.

Variations of this problem

Workers ignore procedures when they become outdated or overly complex and confusing. Their relevance is also undermined when they are poorly written or when audits or reviews are not scheduled, are delayed, or are circumvented. All of these failures unintentionally communicate that they are unimportant.

It's also best to be consistent. Instructing employees to ignore a standard or procedure once to meet a target date implies permission to do so again in the future.

Fixing it and preventing it in future

When we experience a performance deficiency that is due to disregarding one or more of these elements we of course need to ensure it is corrected but at the same time we need to identify the root cause(s). Often the root cause is inattention by those in authority. This neglect is usually in the form of audits, inspections, and reviews not carried out or neglect in not recognizing and praising such efforts when they are done.

As managers we must actively and regularly promote the importance of policies, regulations and standards. More importantly, we must communicate this importance to employees and periodically follow up personally to demonstrate our concern and to reinforce the perceived importance.

➤ Make adherence to procedures, standards etc. one of the expectations that are **communicated to new people**.

➤ **Remind** people from time to time of the importance of these elements.

➤ Conduct periodic **audits** to ensure they are being followed and communicate the results.

➤ Take **prompt action** when a person fails to comply.

➤ Apply appropriate **consequences**, if the problem reoccurs.

➤ Pay close **attention** to increases in the number of customer complaints, corrections, rework, scrap and similar unsatisfactory results and **praise** all improvements in these numbers.

Observations

In Ken Kendall's case, having a clearly defined process didn't prevent the problem but it assisted the owner in quickly identifying where and why it occurred and the steps that required improvement.

When the manager has a "good enough, let it go" attitude, the employees quickly adopt the same approach to their responsibilities and soon anything and everything is "good enough." **Compliance declines in direct proportion to management's lack of attention.**

Procedures and standards exist to ensure a specific level of quality, output, or result. **Their greatest value is realized when they are upgraded in response to a problem and the individuals recognize that this is happening to prevent recurrence.**

CAUTION

Processes, procedures, policies, regulations and standards, while extremely necessary and valuable, have an inherent tendency to also hinder change and innovation. Therefore, management must provide avenues to stimulate creativity and continuous improvement and, when better methods are generated, incorporate them into the existing procedures and standards to maintain the gains.

"It takes years to build a reputation and only a few minutes to ruin it. If you think about that, you'll do things differently."   **– Warren Buffett**

A Smile Break

"Red meat is not bad for you. Blue-green meat, now that's bad for you."   **– Tommy Smothers, Comedian**

Because

4

They Feel
Overwhelmed
and Confused

Why?

Because

No one seems able or willing to prioritize what needs to be done and there is not enough time or resources to do it all. There is no sense of purpose or progress. There are no goals or priorities, simply an endless and overwhelming volume of work.

The first three chapters demonstrate how often change is the catalyst for situations where employees misread or ignore expectations. In the previous chapter we looked at the way in which global factors have made it urgent for employees to understand the importance of performing to specifications. The same forces have accelerated the pace and complexity of change in the workplace. In an era of mergers and acquisitions, of downsizing and "agile" corporations, it's harder than ever to stay focused. It's more difficult for managers to stay in touch with what's really happening in the workplace and there are those few managers whose response to every challenge is simply to ratchet up the demands on their employees.

The Linkage: From attitudes to results

Initially, employees believe that management doesn't realize the overwhelming demands that are being made of them. When these demands are unrelenting and endless, their perception gradually changes to a belief that management does realize but can't or won't take action to provide some relief and additional resources.

They begin to feel like a hamster running on an exercise wheel in a cage, a wheel that never stops and won't until they drop. This evolves into a feeling that management doesn't care about them or what's happening. Allowed to continue, they feel resentment, frustration, and anger. There is no sense of purpose or achievement, because there is no praise, no end, no sense of completion, only more activities, more assignments, more "must-do" items.

Employees usually struggle mightily to do what is asked of them. They have little choice if they want to retain their jobs, and most people genuinely want to meet expectations as a matter of personal pride. However, if there is no relief and conditions continue to deteriorate with little hope of change, employees protect their health and sanity in whatever ways they can. One method is to take "sick days" to relieve the pressure. Other employees, full of resentment, find ways to "get even." Some find subtle ways to slow down the treadmill they're on; others act in anger to sabotage the equipment, the system or the output.

The result is that frustration grows, morale worsens, absenteeism increases, and productivity declines until management takes corrective action.

THE "RED BALL" SOLUTION

The Engineering Department had grown after the company successfully entered the market with a new world-class technology. Rapidly, the product had proven its value, gained acceptance and achieved market dominance. But after 14 years the market was saturated and, as a result, the departmental staff was drastically reduced. Two years later, with a new, aggressive General Manager, they were again bidding on contracts and adding product lines. Everything was "due yesterday." In spite of approved overtime, target dates were being missed. In an attempt to bring order out of chaos, one of the department's managers ordered a rubber stamp and pad and called it the "Red Ball." When a request was urgent it would be stamped with the Red Ball designation. It was effective for about one week, then (you've likely guessed it) everything seemed to have the Red Ball imprint. Back to square one!

The Engineering Department head himself was frustrated but reluctant to ask for more people. He hesitated because the company was still losing money and the new General Manager was aggressively pursuing new business without committing additional resources. The General Manager was new to this division and didn't know what the capabilities and capacities were and he was reluctant to request funds from the corporation until he knew they were absolutely necessary.

A THOUSAND IDEAS – TWO DOZEN PEOPLE

Craig was the recently appointed Sales Manager of a firm producing earth-moving equipment. He was eager, energetic and overflowing with ideas and projects. Craig was ready to conquer the world but without an army! His employees groaned and rolled their eyes when they saw him coming because they knew another request or task was on its way. They soon developed two coping strategies: some simply nodded "yes" and went about doing what they personally considered most important; others were more creative – they developed "Hot Lists." When Craig had a new item, they simply asked him to add it to the list in the appropriate sequence. This meant that although the Hot List was changed every few days it was always focused on the top three priorities.

So there was the problem. Craig didn't know what the staff were capable of achieving and his style was one of "fire-fighting" rather than a "plan the work – work the plan" style.

Why?

It was his nature, his personality and his *modus operandi*, the way things had been at his previous location. Craig was, at heart, a salesman, happiest when talking to customers and impatient with reports, meetings and structure. He did not remain in this position for long.

OPERATION QUICK START

There had been a sale of numerous plants by one corporation to another. This type of transaction often occurs as companies realign their holdings to focus on core business. Tim had been Plant Manager for one of the plants. It had been reduced to a bare-bones operation. When the plant was purchased the new owner asked him to remain as manager. The target was to be back up and running within 90 days. He recruited his management team. A few had been with the company before, others such as the Human Resources Manager and two plant supervisors would be new. Within 30 days he had the people in place and basic equipment operating. Employees were mostly those who had worked for the previous corporate owner.

From experience, Tim felt that the newly assembled leadership, several of whom had no management experience, required training in order to build co-operation and a fully functioning team. He scheduled a course for three hours each week. Topics such as Leadership, Understanding People, Problem Solving, and Goal Setting were included.

Fortunately, the course facilitator took time to meet briefly with individual participants after each session. The managers complained that there were no goals or priorities. When the facilitators discussed their comments with Tim, his response was to extract a large binder from his desk. Flipping through the tabs he pointed out a section for each manager containing the list of goals that each had established.

"What do they mean they don't know?" he asked.

Goals and priorities became the topic for a lively discussion at the next session. The managers agreed that, with Tim's input, they had established goals for the operating year. The complaint was that *Tim's day-to-day assignments and priorities did not seem at all connected to their longer-range goals.* In fact planning was virtually impossible because of Tim's daily changing directives.

Tim, in turn, explained that he was only responding to demands from their Big Three automobile manufacturing customers. These customers would frequently schedule short-notice visits to the plant to discuss quality concerns or progress on new programs. Each visit would disrupt priorities for at least a week as the team prepared to present their reports to the customer representatives.

The managers and many of the employees were not meeting Tim's expectations. Why? Because they felt his expectations were unreasonable and constantly changing. Why? Because Tim was constantly juggling operational problems and customer demands, he became hyperactive, nervous and stressed. He failed his team in what they required most: calm, calculated, committed leadership. He could have accomplished a great deal with an early morning team "huddle" to clarify the day's priorities followed by individual coaching. Tim needed to stay at his "command post" to answer questions and act as a "shock absorber" between the customers and his managers.

When and why does this type of problem occur?

People usually feel overwhelmed and confused when there has been a huge increase in the volume of work due to additional business, new markets, new customers, or new products and services.

It's also likely to happen when management priorities change or there is a major restructuring or downsizing with staff reductions and budget cuts as a consequence.

Temporary difficulties may be due to the time it takes management to assess and rebalance workload and staffing levels after changes in business levels.

The problem persists when management sees cutting staff as the only response to an increasingly competitive market. Staff reductions should be achieved by the elimination of non-value-added activities or by eliminating unprofitable products and operations. At times, management overlooks cost reduction opportunities in areas such as materials, processes, or marketing.

Variations of this problem

You've got this problem when employees feel overworked and overwhelmed and see no reason for it. They may think that management is deliberately withholding information. As a result, they feel undervalued and they believe that management doesn't understand or care about their situation. Finally they come to suspect that management won't take corrective action unless they have no other choice.

Fixing it and preventing it in future

When facing conditions that are chaotic and overwhelming:

- ➤ **Tell the employees that management is aware** of the circumstances and explain the reasons they are occurring.
- ➤ **Prioritize** the activities into weekly or even daily segments.

➤ Make certain that these short-term goals are **realistic** and achievable otherwise the result is a fail-fail scenario which leads to demotivation.

➤ Create some **visual indicator** of completion. That way employees know at the end of the day that certain items were done.

➤ Create a feeling of **"we are in this together"** by being available, encouraging, and supportive.

➤ Develop ways to periodically **acknowledge and celebrate** what has been achieved.

To prevent this type of problem:

➤ **Communicate** the organization's priorities regularly and the reasons they are important and necessary. In times of change and turmoil communicate more frequently, even daily if required.

➤ **Link** annual and monthly goals to current tasks, activities and projects.

➤ **Avoid** adding new projects or programs until you have the time, energy, and resources to contribute appropriately to their success.

➤ **Ask** your direct reports for their major goals, short and long term, and how their activities are contributing to achievement of what needs to happen now, this month, and this year.

➤ If this is a recurring situation, problem-solve to find the **root cause** and eliminate it.

➤ **Observe** those who are struggling and offer coaching and encouragement.

➤ **Celebrate** accomplishments.

Observations

The leader needs to have a clear sense of what his organization must achieve and how it is going to do this. It must include an understanding both of resources and restrictions and the distinction between "must-do" and "want-to-do" priorities.

Employees (and managers too, at times) may feel they are on a treadmill. Endless, all-out activity without any observable progress is wearing and stressful and often leads to "burnout." The reason is twofold: no sense of priority or meaningful purpose and no sense of achievement because nothing is finished or completed.

Would any of us play golf, hockey, basketball, tennis or any other sport if there was no scorekeeping, no records, no standings to measure achievement? Not likely.

"Equitas Unimatus" **Calm in the midst of the storm.**
– mantra for medical students, Dr. William Osler
physician, professor, researcher

A Smile Break

"There are new career opportunities in this company. We have downsized so much deadwood that we now have a shortage."

Because

5

They
Don't Know How
To Do It

Why?

Because

They have never done it before and have not been told or shown how to do it. They either don't try because they are afraid of making a mistake (and appearing stupid to others or being criticized by "the boss") or they do try but create problems.

It makes sense to ensure that your workforce knows how to do its job, but it's not as straightforward as it sounds. Downsizing or restructuring, can bump capable staff into positions they're not trained for or burden them with unfamiliar responsibilities. Rather than admit their inexperience, some devoted workers may just cross their fingers and "give it a try" out of loyalty to a boss who is also overwhelmed by change. A new manager may inherit a team that he's had no hand in hiring or training. He doesn't know *what* they know, assumes they *do* know, and learns the truth when the errors occur.

The Linkage: From attitudes to results

Employees new to their jobs or tasks usually believe it is a positive situation, an opportunity to learn new skills and gain new knowledge. They also believe that someone will tell them how to do the job and then show them how so they can do it quickly and easily.

They have mixed emotions. On one hand they are excited, open, and willing. On the other they have concerns and questions. Will they be able to do what is required and in the way the supervisor or manager wants? Is it acceptable to ask questions without seeming like a slow learner? Will they be able to remember it all? They feel thankful when they are provided with job instructions or other reference materials. They develop a sense of pride and achievement when they receive praise and encouragement.

New people are motivated to do their best and want to be successful. The vast majority will perform well, some slowly and carefully, others quickly and confidently. They need and appreciate feedback on how they are doing, how they can do better, and how they can do it easier.

The results achieved by employees new to their jobs are dependent on their assessment of the manager and the situation. If both seem supportive, the person will be confident; if it seems negative, they will be hesitant.

WHEN "THE BOSS" DOESN'T KNOW

Bob had just agreed to reprint a brochure for the authors because of several errors. He apologized and settled the matter quickly and pleasantly. As we stood up to leave, he said, "Can you spare a few minutes? I've got a problem, maybe you can help." He explained that he and his wife had purchased the business just the year before and were having difficulties with quality and prompt delivery. "I know the customers," he said, "because I worked for the previous owners for five years as their only sales person. But I don't know enough about running the shop. Now my wife, our bookkeeper and our supervisors are telling me that I've got the jobs all screwed up."

Bob asked if we could come in, talk to his people and find out what he needed to do. At the same time, he asked if we could suggest what training his supervisors might need.

The following week each person was interviewed. During the interview, each staff member had similar complaints. They reported that Bob didn't like to see people "standing around" so he would suggest they go help someone else. If the customer service person seemed idle, he would tell them to help one of the supervisors or his wife who handled the hiring and credits and collections. The result was chaos because no one was sure what he or she should be doing. None of the supervisors, including Bob and his wife, had ever received any supervisory or management training. There were no instructions, no procedures, no in-house "expert" they could turn to for answers.

Supervisors also complained that employee turnover was so high they felt it was a waste of time to train new people. Even if they had wanted to, no one had ever taught them how to properly train employees.

Bob's wife, Wilma did all of the hiring as well as credits and collections. She agreed that turnover was much too high. Often new people would start with the company but quit after a couple of weeks, or even after a day or two.

"This place is a zoo," some of the departing employees would comment, "totally disorganized."

"I can get another job paying more money," others would say. Wilma was frustrated. With no previous experience in hiring she was simply doing the best she could to help her husband. She agreed that wage levels were too low to attract and keep good people, but Bob had told her they couldn't afford to pay more. So she struggled on, doing her best given the circumstances.

It was obvious that all five of the people we spoke to sincerely wanted to be more effective and knew improvements were needed. They were frustrated and willing to try anything that could make a difference. The situation was like a logjam: the issues so intertwined that freeing the flow of work through the shop seemed impossible.

After the interviews were completed Bob was naturally anxious to know what had been said. We reviewed the issues we had uncovered:

1. Responsibilities were overlapping, and therefore confusing.
2. No one in leadership roles had been trained or had prior experience.
3. There was high employee turnover.
4. There was no structured hiring process and Wilma was inexperienced.
5. The wage rates were too low to attract and keep good people.
6. Everyone was frustrated, anxious for improvements, and willing to help.
7. Customer complaints were frequent and rework and replacement costs were high.
8. These issues were affecting profitability.

As we talked through the list, Bob nodded in agreement. When we finished, he asked for further help. Starting that same day, we listed the shop's five jobs and key responsibilities on a flipchart in terms of expected results, activities and tasks. When the chart was completed Bob asked, for a meeting to show it to the supervisors and see if they agreed. He did just that and they did agree. Then Bob shared with them the list of issues which had been developed and asked if there were any changes they would suggest to the list. They said no, it was complete. He promised swift action and thanked them for being so willing to share their frustrations. They, in turn, thanked him for listening and making the first moves. They promised to help in any way they could.

This meeting was followed by supervisory training one evening a week for ten weeks. Everyone participated including Wilma and Bob. "I need this as much as anyone," said Bob. This attitude and his participation generated a tight bond in the group. In the course of their training, the supervisors developed work instructions for every job.

Wage rates were increased. Bob was finally convinced that paying more and reducing the turnover rate and therefore reducing the quality and delivery problems would actually *improve* profitability. Wilma received one-on-one coaching in the hiring process including interviewing, checking references and testing. She also developed a chart to monitor turnover trends.

As result of these changes, turnover was reduced by 78 percent. Customer complaints dropped 92 percent while profits rose 60 percent. It took Bob and his team just 120 days to completely turn the company around.

Let's use Bob's case to revisit some of the tools we discussed in this book's Getting Started section. It's an excellent opportunity to use the"Probe For Cause" process in which we repeatedly pose the question "Why?" We start here with the result that was troubling Bob:

There were frequent customer complaints.	Why?
Because of quality and delivery problems.	Why?
The employees were making errors.	Why?
They hadn't been properly trained.	Why?
The supervisors didn't know how and felt it was a waste of time.	Why?
Management (Bob) didn't know how to train his supervisors. He believed that low wage rates would ensure profitability.	Why?
He had no previous experience in supervision and no education in business management.	Why?
It wasn't required for his previous duties, which were in sales.	

We can also analyze Bob's situation using the Performance Model from the Getting Started section. A lack of business education and experience led to his **attitude** that low wages were the key to profitability and that people should know what to do. This led to **emotions** (frustration with the supervisors) that led to his **actions** (forcing key people to jump in to others' duties in an effort to keep everyone busy, then blaming the supervisors for not training their people).

The **tangible results** were unsatisfactory profits, frequent customer complaints, scrap, rework and high employee turnover. The **intangible results** were high levels of frustration among the supervisors, the employees and in Bob himself, also a lack of co-operation, and an atmosphere of blame and resentment. These negative experiences were a factor in the continuation of these problems.

When and why does this type of problem occur?

People may not know how to do what you expect when they are in new positions or when the way the work must be done is altered due to changes in materials or processes or for other reasons.

The individual may not know how to do what's expected due to lack of previous experience and a lack of training.

Variations of this problem

If employees are not performing to your expectations, it may be that they don't know how to do the job. They may not thoroughly understand their responsibilities. Employees may wonder if a task is their job or someone else's. If they haven't done the job for some months, they may have forgotten the proper steps and do tasks out of sequence. They may not know what to do if there's a problem or if they themselves make a mistake.

Fixing it and preventing it in future

When a performance problem occurs and you ask, "What happened?" the employee may say, "I didn't know what to do" or "I didn't know how to handle this, I've never had to do this before." Corrective action is simple:

➤ **Tell** them how, **show** them how, and have them **do** it.
➤ **Compliment** them on what they have done properly and correct any errors by saying, "It's easier and more effective if you do this or do it this way."
➤ Before leaving, take time to ask, "Is there **anything else** that you've been wondering about or uncertain about?" This allows them an opportunity to raise any other issues or questions.

To prevent these problems:

➤ **Train every employee** at every level to do the work safely, correctly, efficiently and to quality standards.
➤ **Use a non-threatening, capable person** (from inside or outside the organization) to do the training.
➤ **Provide work instructions** that are easy to understand, correct and up-to-date.
➤ Ensure that **safety, customer satisfaction, quality and waste reduction** are the focus for everyone.
➤ Support training wholeheartedly by **getting personally involved.**
➤ **Use appropriate resources**: job instruction by a respected and well liked internal candidate; outside trainers who can bring new knowledge and skills to the organization; a coach/mentor for individuals who will benefit from one-on-one coaching; courses, seminars, workshops on specific topics that relate to your organization's needs.

➤ **Implement a documented process** that ensures every employee is properly instructed and trained before assigning new responsibilities.

➤ **Audit the process** at regular intervals to confirm that it is being followed, is effective and up to date.

➤ When problems occur due to lack of effective training, use them as opportunities to **review and improve the process.**

➤ **Keep all training practical**. Develop doable, significant skills.

➤ Training sessions often unearth opportunities for improvement. **Ask trainers to provide feedback**.

➤ Training should **include a requirement for prompt, on-the-job application** of the knowledge and skills gained to increase retention and to build effective habits.

➤ **Develop an evaluation** of training that tells you *what* they have learned and *how well* they have learned it, that shows whether they can *apply* what they've learned and are applying it. Your evaluation should measure whether they have achieved improved results, whether the organization has benefited and to what extent.

Effective training usually generates intangible benefits as well, such as improved co-operation, greater teamwork, better understanding. In your follow-up to a training program, determine whether this has happened.

Observations

If we fail to train people who are facing a new situation, we send the unintended message that we don't care about performance or their frustrations. Eventually this can lead to de-motivation.

Learning by trial and error used to be the method most frequently used. Now it is the least used because it is the costliest. Learning by trial and error results in scrap, rework, customer complaints and lost business.

Avoid using the question, "Can you do…?" Usually the employee will answer, "Yes." Even if they can't do what's expected. Instead ask, "Would you like someone to show you how to do this task?" If they answer, "That's not necessary," verify their ability by asking them to tell you and show you how they would do it.

There are times in every organization when no one knows what to do or how best to do it. This is usually due to changes in conditions, processes, or people. That's when it's most cost-effective and efficient to bring in an external trainer or consultant.

"I hear and I forget, I see and I remember, I do and I understand."   – **Confucius**

"Through some very sophisticated research, we now know the motivation for mastery – the desire to feel effective – exists from earliest infancy."
– **David W. Krueger, MD, Author,** *Emotional Business*

A Smile Break

Learning by trial and error

"With six brothers, I learned to dance waiting to use the bathroom.

"I gave up my early boxing career because the referees kept stepping on my hands."

- Bob Hope

Employees Not Doing What You Expect

Because

6 They Don't Have The
Resources

Why?

Because

The resources are not available or they are deficient, defective, or delayed beyond the required time. These resources may be any or all of the following: materials, supplies, tools, equipment, software, finances, people, decisions, approvals, or information.

There's an old parable that tells of how for want of a nail, a shoe was lost, how for want of a shoe a horse was lost, how for want of a horse a rider was lost and how for want of a rider, the battle was lost. The parable underlines how important it is that managers understand what their people need to get the job done. Sometimes the most fundamental requirements can, at first glance, appear to be frills or indulgences.

The Linkage: From Attitudes to Results

Employees who are willing and able to do what is required, assume and expect that they will be provided with the resources they need to efficiently do their work. When this isn't the case, their attitudes vary, depending on the frequency and seriousness of the deficiencies. If it seldom happens, they accept it and work as best they can. If it's frequent, regular, and serious, they begin to believe that management either doesn't care, or that management is inept or ignoring the situation. In either case they lose confidence and respect for management and for the system.

Conscientious people find it frustrating when they can't be effective. Delays and defects in resources make their tasks and activities more difficult. They resent the extra effort required and doubt management's commitment to their responsibilities. "They don't care," they start to say to themselves. "Why should I care?" Even the most dedicated employee eventually gives up being concerned or making extra effort when they come to the conclusion that the situation is unlikely to change. Therefore they "do what they have to do," knowing full well that their productivity and the effectiveness of the organization could be much improved if "management did what management is paid to do."

When resources are not available, or are deficient or defective, it has a negative impact on efficiency, productivity and quality.

GIVE THEM WHAT THEY NEED

Sarah was assigned as supervisor to a custom machining department with the specific instruction to focus on improving productivity. After just a few days, she realized that a lot of time was being lost by employees searching for drawings, material, process information, and cutting tools. She initiated a system to ensure that all drawings and process information were placed in a package the day before they were needed. Next she arranged for tooling information to be available two days before required. Material availability was assigned to the production controller with the exhortation to "make it a priority" to have material at the machines when needed. Productivity increased by 29 percent within three months and so did employee morale.

The machinists finally had a supervisor who was committed to providing them with all of the resources they needed to be effective and efficient.

LACK OF SUPPORT

In the Human Resources Department, a young lady often complained of neck pain. Her doctor recommended that she request a special chair that would provide better back support. The director of the department nixed the request, saying, "If I order a special chair for you there will be dozens of similar requests." She struggled on, using pain-killers. Finally she had to change employers.

The loss in productivity from this person and the cost of recruiting and training a replacement were higher by far than the cost of a chair would have been. It also created the impression among other employees that people and their concerns were unimportant.

DEFECTIVE INFORMATION EQUALS PROFIT LOSS

Eric, the president of a roof truss manufacturing company and his brother Paul struggled with meager profits in an extremely competitive market. Both felt that much of the problem was due to their young supervisors who lacked experience. So they arranged for in-plant leadership training with the authors as facilitators.

During the second training session, we questioned the company supervisors and managers concerning production error rates.

"As a guesstimate," we asked, "what percentage of your time and effort and those of your employees is spent in correcting, changing or replacing your output because of incorrect information from the sales department or directly from the customer?"

The answers ranged from 25 percent to 45 percent. The president audibly gasped and said, "My God, that's got to be costing us a million dollars, and that's profit dollars."

Eliminating even some of this wasted effort could easily have doubled or tripled the company's profit. For the balance of that session the president was lost in thought. Although physically present, he couldn't participate. His mind was elsewhere. Beginning the next day and ever since, his pursuit of those savings has been both relentless and successful.

Why wasn't the company more profitable? Why weren't the employees more productive? Because they lacked the correct information they needed from the customers. Adding to the problem was the fact that the company's accounting information was inadequate. It did not provide management with proper cost data regarding losses, errors and defects.

Finally, it was because the president and his brother didn't realize what these frequent omissions and errors were costing the company.

When does this type of problem occur?

Once again, change is often the root cause when people find themselves short of the resources they require. Their work can be short circuited by any of the following:

> A significant or unexpected increase or decrease in volume and systems that are no longer suitable to the change in demand.

> Changes in materials, suppliers, customer specifications that occur without warning or preparation.

> Employee transitions, with new people in new jobs who have not been effectively trained.

➤ Organizational alterations in structure, reporting, or priorities and a lack of understanding of processes and needs.

The situation can occur during emergency situations due to a lack or deficiency of planning and employee training for these occasions.

The reasons why this type of problem occurs may include:

➤ A procurement and scheduling process that is overly complex, involving many suppliers, and other elements that provide multiple opportunities for something to go wrong.

➤ Arbitrary decisions by those in control that the employee or department doesn't really need the item(s) requested. Sometimes such decisions are made with insufficient information or without an understanding of the impact on customers and employees.

Variations of this problem

Employees lack the resources to do the job when the materials, supplies, tools or equipment required are delayed or defective. They're deprived of what they need when information is incorrect, incomplete or late. They can be left short of all these requirements when budgets do not provide sufficient funds or when approvals and decisions are postponed or become so difficult to obtain they reduce lead times and time available for implementation

Fixing and preventing this problem in future

When employees say that they haven't got what they need, take action **promptly**. Delays usually cause productivity problems and negatively impact the motivation of the personnel struggling with this deficiency. Be conscious of the fact that the people closest to a situation usually have the best knowledge of what is needed and why. If you are unsure that the resources truly are required, or if it involves a significant cost or other investment, schedule a **brainstorming** session to generate a number of alternatives, evaluate them, and select the best. Ask the affected workers to **prioritize** their requirements, to specify the timeframe and to explain why.

Finally, do everything necessary to put the needed resources in the hands of those who have to get the job done.

In order to ensure shortages don't happen again:

> ➤ **Anticipate** resource needs in advance.
> ➤ **Be alert to difficulties** caused by a lack of resources, correcting the situation usually eliminates a bottleneck and improves productivity rapidly.
> ➤ When reducing budgets or cutting costs which could affect resource availability, **use proven methods** such as Value Analysis or Process Redesign to ensure that only non-value-added functions are being eliminated.
> ➤ When significant changes are planned, use a **team-based approach** to identify and avoid potential resource problems by considering the **total process** and not just one element.
> ➤ Arrange to have most or all resources provided as **one unit delivered at the same time.**
> ➤ **Problem-solve instances of resource unavailability**, get to the root cause and make permanent changes to eliminate recurrence.

Observations

Resource problems result in frustrated in-house personnel and reduced effectiveness. They often negatively impact the end customer as well.

Most resource problems are the result of process deficiencies, management decisions, planning defects or changed circumstances. Tracking these problems down and eliminating them usually results in significant payback and improved morale.

> *Problems can be like the grains of sand in an oyster – they can result in a pearl of great value.*
>
> **– The Authors**

A Smile Break

Judge: Well sir, judging from your answer on how you reacted to the emergency, it sounds like you're a person of intelligence and good judgment.

Witness: Thank you, Your Honour. If I weren't under oath, I'd return the compliment.

Because

7

They Are Being
Prevented By Others

Why?

Because

One or more informal or formal group leaders are deliberately limiting the employees' work effort and output. These leaders may be doing it simply to demonstrate their power and influence to others in the work group or to the manager. Their motivations could be personal or stem from a labor dispute.

The employees have been well trained and given the tools they need. They know what's expected of them and they want to do the job right. But some may be afraid to raise the hackles of co-workers who don't like being "shown up" by those who do their work thoroughly and well.

These individuals may want to test a new manager's expectations and tolerance level, get him or her to ease up on certain demands or overlook unacceptable behaviors and practices. Sometimes, it is done in retaliation for certain actions the manager has initiated or to "soften-up" what they consider a "hard-nosed" new manager.

Pressuring others to do the minimum could be a ploy to force management to schedule overtime that pays one-and-a-half or double time. Or it could just be a game, a way to overcome boredom and have some "fun" at the expense of the supervisor or manager. Some individuals express their creativity by attempting to "beat the system" or torment "the boss," enlisting others in these efforts.

Withholding effort or "working to rule" is a recognized tactic used by unions and professional associations to create a public outcry, speed up the bargaining process and hopefully gain a more generous settlement. Work-to-rule is often part of union strategy prior to or during contract negotiations to bring pressure to bear on the employer's negotiating team.

The Linkage: From attitudes to results

Employees who are motivated and want to perform well are at times confronted by conflicting pressures and loyalties. They want to do their jobs to the best of their abilities. However, they are also members of a work group, professional association or a union, and are expected to comply with group norms.

They believe they have little choice but to do what their co-workers, associations or unions dictate, even if they are adamantly opposed. Caught between two opposing forces they usually feel they must fit in with their group, follow the instructions of their leadership and hope to make it up to management later through their job performance.

The few who are demotivated, distrustful, and negative view it as an opportunity to "punish" the company and management, demonstrate their power, and do it with the support of similar-minded work group members who are informal leaders.

When changes are being implemented by management, these few believe that what management is doing or intends to do is potentially detrimental to them in terms of effort or income.

Usually one or more formal or informal leaders exploit such beliefs and convince others that they need to "flex their muscles," demonstrate their power and send management a "wake-up call."

Capable and motivated workers are disappointed and frustrated by conditions out of their control. They want to please both parties, which is usually difficult if not impossible. Again, those who are disruptive and distrustful vent their anger and blame management for the situation. Their predominant emotions are suspicion and skepticism. They are wary of anything that management proposes suspecting some adverse effect or trap.

Those considered the best, most reliable people will "hunker down," and "keep a low profile." They do what they can to satisfy their manager but don't do anything opposed by their association or union. They take the same stance with the union, they will walk the picket line or withhold their services if they absolutely must, but will engage in the least provocative actions possible.

The disruptive individuals we consider our challenges are usually aware of the actions and behaviors that will or will not be tolerated by management. However, the extremists in this group, intentionally or unintentionally emboldened by the rhetoric of their union or association, may go as far as to assault replacement workers, supervisors, or fellow workers who they judge to be less militant. Those with destructive tendencies sabotage in-process product or damage company property.

The results are that the productivity is usually reduced. Occasionally there are work stoppages and, in a few instances, there are personal injuries and property damage until the parties resolve the issues.

ROWING FOR BRONZE

It may not be a co-worker who holds a good performer back, but a supervisor or manager who, consciously or unconsciously, fears the consequences of success.

Difficult though it is to believe, there are coaches who would rather have their teams win a bronze medal or finish fourth instead of winning the gold. According to the coach of a university rowing team, some coaches prefer third place because it's a comfortable, acceptable finish, one that allows for an improvement the next year. If they win the gold they are concerned that they will be asked two questions they would rather avoid: "Why didn't we achieve this last year?" and "Will the team win gold again next year?" Winning gold raises expectations.

Managers and employees sometimes attempt to lower the expectations of others so that they can demonstrate future improvement when necessary to retain their position.

HELP INSTEAD OF HINDRANCE

With just three weeks to go before the labor contract was to expire, the company was behind in production and in danger of being late delivering units to its largest and long-time customer. The only way to catch up and meet the date was to schedule significant overtime. Expecting resistance or outright refusal, management had no alternative but to ask the union's Plant Chairman to support the request for overtime and recommend approval to the membership. The timing couldn't have been much worse, the employees had already voted in favor of a strike (not unusual as it increases the leadership's bargaining power), and relations between management and the union were strained to say the least.

But management explained that both the company and the employees would benefit from satisfying the customer and therefore ensuring a continuing relationship. Even at this time of high tension, both sides were able to set aside their differences and recognize the mutual benefit in satisfying the customer.

When and why does this type of problem occur?

People are most frequently hindered by others in meeting expectations on one of these four occasions:

1. When a new "eager-beaver" employee is hired and is making a greater effort and producing more than existing people in the department.
2. When a new manager is appointed some employees may reduce their effort, extend break periods, or attempt short cuts to determine whether the manager will accept this level of activity.
3. At a time of change in rules, practices, pay, benefits, workload, hours of work, new equipment or processes, informal leaders will carefully scrutinize the changes to determine any possible negative impact.
4. During contract negotiations or during labor disputes over grievances, as noted above, there will be some who restrict their personal efforts and those of others.

Deliberate restriction of the effort of others is usually a "power play." It is intended to demonstrate to the new employee, to others in the work group, to management or to all three, where the power lies. The purpose is to achieve one of two goals: it's either to gain some benefit, payoff, or concession or to punish management for some change or penalty they have introduced.

Variations of this problem

You may have this problem when you see groups deliberately avoiding interaction with an individual in the workplace. It may come to your attention when physical threats and/or attacks on those willing to work are reported. It can rear its head in numerous ways during times of labor unrest (work-to-rule campaigns, restrictions on voluntary activities, picket lines and union-imposed penalties on members who violate these sanctions).

Fixing it and preventing it in future

Whenever a new employee joins your area, be alert to possible pressures to limit output and the possibility that some employees may abuse or "haze" the new person. At the first sign that this is happening, take prompt action:

➣ If one of your informal leaders is constantly creating dissention, **discuss the situation with your Human Resources people** and ask for their suggestions and support. Then take appropriate corrective disciplinary action. Additional information in Chapter 12 will be helpful.

➣ In some instances a **transfer** for the individual may be a viable solution (*but never to a more desirable or higher paying position or you will be seen as rewarding the negative behavior*). A transfer should serve only to isolate the individual and minimize their impact, never to shift the problem to some other manager.

➣ Whatever you do, **do not ignore the situation** because you will, by your inaction, be condoning and perpetuating the behavior.

Employees are constantly, consciously or unconsciously, assessing their manager, their fellow employees, and the situation. It occurs automatically and continually. It affects their attitudes, emotions, and behavior. They decide where their loyalties are best served and who has credibility, whom they can trust and respect. An astute manager prevents disruptive elements from getting the upper hand by gaining the support of his workforce. He does this by communicating and acting in a caring and consistent manner:

> ➤ Winning employees to your way of thinking and gaining their loyalty is best achieved by **eliminating negative conditions**. The effort begins with communicating expectations and ensuring employees know how to do the job. When you take the time and make the effort to do this, you build the foundation for a lasting relationship of cooperation, loyalty, trust, and respect.
> ➤ Management can frequently prevent this type of problem by **communicating promptly and frankly their reasons for any significant change**, why it is necessary, and how it is beneficial to the employees, the company, and the customers.

Observations

In union conflicts and negotiating situations, the individual manager is limited in what can be done personally to mitigate the influence of those restricting performance. However, virtually every contract contains a "notwithstanding clause." These clauses state that, other than those contract provisions in the agreement, "management has the exclusive right to manage the business."

The manager faces the challenge to remain focused and carry on in the normal firm-but-fair manner. Avoid arguments, accusations, and ignore rumors at times of labor unrest. When the pot is boiling, don't fan the flames. Remain calm, quietly support management efforts, get the work done, and show appreciation for employee efforts.

Remind employees that at some point all contentious issues will be settled and an agreement will be reached. Mention the fact that, no matter what happens, both the company and the union must satisfy the customers or there will be no company and no jobs. Job security depends on the company, its employees, and the customers who must be satisfied.

"If you want to test a man's character, give him power."
- Abraham Lincoln

"If you're going through hell, keep going."
- Winston Churchill

A Smile Break

"Learn from the mistakes of others. You can't live long enough to make them all yourself."
- Anonymous

Because

8

They
Aren't Suited
To The Job

Why?

Because

Their physical, mental or emotional characteristics (which might be ideal for certain positions) hinder or prevent their effectiveness in this particular position. With others, their values differ from those of the organization, manager or work group. Therefore they at times feel internal conflict and, in extreme cases, find it impossible to work for the organization or with their colleagues.

Your gut feeling about a person says, "Hire them!" Their resumé is great. In interviews they show a good grasp of the job's requirements, but more important, they exude a certain something that you feel your company is lacking, the "razzle dazzle" you feel the sales force needs, or an air of calm professionalism that will be a good influence on others in the office. You give them the job and nothing turns out the way you expected. What happened?

The Linkage: From attitudes to results

Sprinters are physically different from marathon runners, artists are different from accountants, and investors are more cautious than speculators. **These differences do not make one person "better" than the other. It means they are usually "better suited" for certain tasks, functions, and responsibilities**.

They think they can do what's needed and may blame their shortcomings on others or circumstances. A few feel they are overqualified for the position and its requirements. On a subconscious level, they realize they just don't fit – this job truly isn't for them.

They usually feel frustrated and unhappy because they're having difficulty. They need the job so they struggle to do what's required. Some feel overwhelmed and stressed. A few feel bored because the job doesn't interest or challenge them and they're not good at it.

The behaviors you may observe range from avoidance, (expressed in absenteeism), excuses for below par performance and blaming the circumstances, the processes and other people. Effort is often half-hearted because they begin to realize that they cannot or do not truly want to perform to the levels required.

Surveys conducted over many years typically report that as many as 65 percent of employees dislike the jobs they hold. They remain in their positions for a number of reasons: the pay, the benefits, the prestige afforded by the position, the title, or the potential opportunities. The more intangible reasons include lack of other perceived opportunities, family responsibilities, low self-esteem, or fear of making a change.

The result is they are not happy. Their performance is below par and, of course, you are not happy. It's truly a lose-lose situation.

The ideal condition is one in which the people are interested in their jobs, challenged by the nature of what has to be accomplished and able to utilize their natural talents. Therefore, they perform well and so they experience the emotional benefits that naturally accrue from good performance: a sense of achievement, pride in their accomplishments, the respect of their peers and the recognition and praise of their manager. This is an enviable win-win situation.

TRADING PLACES

Laura and Anne both held positions in Human Resources. Laura was a coordinator in the Training Department and enjoyed the needs identification work, the preparation and development aspects of the job, as well as interacting with senior management in other departments. Anne was a clerk in the Benefits Section, where procedures and policies were clearly defined and the only decision making allowed was whether a claim was or was not eligible for payment. Both women were excellent performers, well educated and interested in opportunities that could lead to promotion.

Individually, over a period of several months, they made known their interest in a job change to broaden their experience base.

The Human Resources Director, thinking he would make both happy, agreed to a job exchange between the two. Unfortunately, none of the trio involved gave enough thought to the differences in the requirements of these two positions or differences in the preferences, interests and personality characteristics of the two applicants. Within 60 days, both requested to return to their former duties. Anne felt very uncomfortable in an unstructured situation where she had to collect, develop, and identify what needed to be done. She much preferred definition, rules, and clear-cut guidelines from which to make decisions. Laura was similarly unhappy with the confining rules and regulations in the Benefits Section.

There were gains from the experiment. Both women were more satisfied with their original positions once they returned. Both became better HR members having had a taste of the stress endured by individuals stuck in jobs they don't enjoy. They also learned that, while they certainly could handle the new duties, they were not suited to each other's jobs because of their personality characteristics and preferences. They both came to appreciate how little most people understand about their own characteristics and which positions best suit their natural talents and preferences. The exchange served as a demonstration of how skillful those making hiring and placement decisions must be when it comes to determining a job candidate's suitability.

CHAINSAW

Business publications have reported the many twists and turns in Chainsaw's career. They say he had earned the dubious honor of this name because of his executive methods. The Board of Directors for an internationally known small kitchen appliance producer hired him as CEO because they wanted someone who would stem the flow of red ink and restore their company to growth and profitability. Chainsaw's slash-and-burn tactics at a previous corporation had been legendary and effective and the Board fully expected he would return their company to profitability quickly.

According to press accounts, Chainsaw began to use the same aggressive approaches that had created his reputation. Only this time he made the cuts more quickly and deeply. Month by month, board members became more uncertain about the wisdom of their decision to hire Chainsaw. With his characteristic enthusiasm, energy, and absolute conviction, Chainsaw began to dismember (downsize) the company. Before long, the corporate patient's health deteriorated and began an accelerated decline. Difficult as it was to do, the board finally decided they had made a mistake and chopped Chainsaw from his position. The damage he had done to the lives of employees and to the welfare of the company was impossible to estimate.

It was reported that, as his approach failed to yield the desired results, Chainsaw doctored the company's books to make things appear better than they were. Charged with security fraud by the Securities and Exchange Commission, he agreed to pay a $500,000 penalty. In shareholder lawsuits, investors won a $110 million settlement from the appliance maker. Chainsaw reportedly paid $15 million of this amount.

It all happened because of one hiring decision gone wrong. The corporation's bankruptcy reorganization plan was finally approved and shortly after, it changed its name.

On the surface, the board got exactly what it wanted: a person who would aggressively tackle the profit problem. What the board members didn't anticipate was the possibility that the selected candidate would go too far with his extreme measures. Their initial confidence in Chainsaw was absolute and their realization of what was actually happening came too late.

ACQUIRING A NEW PURCHASING DIRECTOR

The General Manager had developed a suspicion over the past year that one reason for his company's skimpy profits was the performance of the purchasing agent. Purchased materials accounted for almost a third of product cost and he hadn't seen any new strategies or tactics to reduce these costs. Fortunately, the incumbent was due to retire, giving the General Manager an opportunity to search for a new, aggressive, dynamic individual. To reflect the importance of the position and justify a higher salary rate he changed the title to Purchasing Director and instructed the Human Resources Department to enlist the help of a search firm.

Because of the generous compensation package offered, a candidate was quickly identified and hired. The General Manager boasted to his Executive Committee that he had lured a person with experience managing a department of six people.

Within four months, the new recruit left the company. He hadn't realized that, while his new position offered a great title and excellent rewards, he had no employees to manage except for a shared clerk. In this job he was no longer a manager of staff but a "doer," talking to salespeople and issuing purchase orders. In addition, he discovered that most of his purchased material dollars went to three major steel companies who would not yield on their prices.

Could the new Director of Purchasing have done what the General Manager expected? He didn't think so and he considered the job beneath him even though the salary was attractive. Both parties misjudged the importance of prestige in this situation and it was a deal breaker. The General Manager in his haste and enthusiasm oversold the challenges and opportunities afforded by the position. The candidate allowed himself to be seduced by the title and the salary and should have asked more questions regarding staffing and performance expectations.

THE MOTORCYCLE GANG

A large manufacturer landed a lucrative contract that stipulated an almost impossible delivery date. Management and employees rushed to complete drawings and issue orders for long-lead-time materials. Left to last was deciding how many additional plant employees would be required.

With only two weeks before production start, Human Resources were finally given a requisition for 35 highly qualified welders and a number of less skilled assembly workers. Unfortunately, high employment levels in the area meant that welders were extremely difficult to find. Time was of the essence, so Human Resources simply hired anyone who indicated they had held a welding torch. In the rush to find applicants, welding tests and reference checks with previous employers were bypassed.

No one realized that six motorcycle gang members were among those employed in the stampede to hire. As you might guess, during their probationary period, they were model employees with never a problem. Shortly after the end of the period they began loan sharking and soon they were dealing drugs. It took months of concerted effort by Human Resources and the supervisors involved to identify, document, and apply the disciplinary steps required to discharge the six.

Could the bikers have done what was expected? Of course they could have, but they weren't there for the paycheck. They had a more lucrative trade in mind. Their values, behaviors, and intentions were unsuitable for the job and the company.

The root cause of this situation was management's faulty planning and delays which yielded insufficient lead time to find appropriate candidates.

CHUCK'S TREASURE

When his father retired, Chuck took over the family tool and die shop. Under Dad's direction, the business had grown from the original three people to the current twenty-four. On average, they hired one new person a year and sometimes two. Hiring was never a problem because the company had a fine reputation in the community. The company paid well, and communicated openly with the employees. Because of his hands-on experience with every piece of equipment while working side-by-side with the employees, Chuck found it an easy task to evaluate the technical skills of job applicants. If he was unsure after interviewing an individual, he simply took them out to the shop and had them demonstrate their ability. Soon after Chuck took over the company, it began an enviable growth curve. He hired a new person every second month or more often.

That's when the problems began to appear. Most frequently, the problem was not with the new hire's ability to perform the tasks but with less obvious elements such as work effort, attendance, the ability to work with others, the ability to learn, to problem solve and multitask.

Chuck recognized his personal need for training in the areas of interviewing and selection skills. To his credit, he completed an extension course at the local community college. But he still lacked confidence and began talking to colleagues and consultants in a search that led him to what he later called his "Treasure." It was a relatively simple paper and pencil questionnaire that evaluated a number of applicant abilities, interests, and personality characteristics. One of the features he most appreciated was the results printout which provided both a narrative comment on each element in the assessment form and a numerical weighting to indicate the extent the applicant possessed each characteristic.

To develop his skill in using this tool, Chuck filled it out himself. To test it further, he asked his key people if they would complete the assessment. Soon he had everyone with the company complete it, including his son and daughter.

An assessment document such as Chuck's has a variety of benefits. It provides important information that is difficult if not impossible to gain from a resumé or an interview (such as a measurable assessment of a candidate's interests and motivation). It either confirms or conflicts with what has been learned in the interview and therefore leads to additional questions for a second interview.

The ability to effectively evaluate job applicants and employees seeking promotion is one of a leader's vital skills. It prevents problems before they occur. It results in improved hiring therefore avoiding the stress, and costs associated with ineffective recruiting. Sound hiring decisions generally lead to better productivity, motivation and morale.

When and why does this type of problem occur?

Unfortunately managers usually realize that a person is unsuited to a position shortly *after* that person has been hired, transferred or promoted to new responsibilities. The problem can also arise when a new manager has been appointed to head the department and expectations change. An employee can suddenly become unsuited to a position they've handled quite capably when the job itself changes in terms of tasks involved, technical requirements or level of difficulty.

When a company is downsizing, people may be shifted into positions that don't suit them. The same thing can happen when a company enjoys rapid growth and individuals are promoted before their current performance, true capabilities, or suitability have been evaluated.

At times, it occurs because the person doing the hiring hasn't totally understood the job requirements, or special aspects of the situation. It may be that they were too hurried or inexperienced to be effective in the interviewing and selection process. In some cases the candidate claims to have done this type of job previously when they haven't.

In some instances transfers and promotions are made on the basis of seniority or other reasons and not on ability and interests.

Finally, many faulty selection decisions are made because the person in charge hasn't followed all of the selection steps or has no proven method to test for one or more of the required attributes. Every organization is more effective in hiring when it uses an effective evaluation method, one that measures the ability to learn and problem solve, ranks a candidates interest in numbers, people, or things, and evaluates essential personality characteristics. Without this type of tool there is an over-reliance on "gut feel," the resumé, the interview process, or the reference checks which themselves may or may not be reliable.

Variations of this problem

There are many ways in which a worker can prove unsuitable for a position. Some are better at working with their hands than their head. It could be that they learn and think too slowly to problem solve quickly in rapid response situations or they may be better at completing one task at a time rather than work on multiple tasks concurrently. There are those who prefer a slow steady pace rather than a fast-paced situation.

People can be surprising too; they can show ability with numbers, words or objects yet lack an interest in tasks requiring these abilities.

It may also be a matter of values. There are those who prefer to work alone rather than in a team. Some people would rather cooperate than compete. They may even believe it is unethical or immoral to sell or persuade others, which makes them unsuitable for sales positions.

Fixing and preventing it in future

Before deciding whether an individual is or is not suited to a position, management should have had several discussions with the employee. Do not begin your conversation with the question, "Why did you do this?" or "Why aren't you doing this?" A "why" question at this stage will likely be viewed as criticism and will result in a defensive response instead of useful information. Instead use open ended questions or simple statements such as, "Tell me what happened," or "Tell me what's giving you difficulty and what you enjoy."

It is important to have reviewed the expectations, provided training, ensured that required resources were available, and to have conducted several coaching sessions to provide the person every opportunity to perform satisfactorily.

The employee must have been cautioned that continued unsatisfactory performance would lead to termination. They must have had the opportunity to explain their sub-par performance. If these steps have been taken and it has been determined that the individual is not suited to the position based on performance, you then have several options:

> If the deficiency is minor and/or the duties are temporary, it may be best to **leave** the person in the position.
> In some cases it may be best to **transfer** them to another position where they are better suited, more qualified and able to be more effective. (This should never be done to simply move the problem to some other manager.)
> If this is not a viable option, it is at times best for all if the person **finds more suitable employment elsewhere**. Some organizations assist in this process by offering a termination settlement and/or out-placement counselling. When this is done carefully and effectively the result is usually that the person finds a position where they are more productive, less stressed, happier and more successful. Always be aware of the organization's procedures and past practices and the legal requirements before initiating action.

To avoid putting people into jobs for which they are not suitable, a selection process is required that includes these elements:

> A **summary of the requirements** for the job being filled. What tasks have to be performed? What decisions will have to be made? What are the most difficult challenges the person will face and how frequently will they occur? What knowledge and skills will the person require? What personality characteristics are *desirable* and which are a *must?* What are the conditions they will have to function in, not only environmentally, but also in terms of speed, pressure, accuracy, and relationships?

➤ A **job application form** that gathers essential information and meets governmental regulations.

➤ Always **request a resumé** as it provides an overall summary from the applicant's viewpoint. Resumés, unfortunately, have lost much of their value as a source of accurate information because some applicants tend to exaggerate, generalize or intentionally deceive. Many candidates have a company or a friend prepare their resumé. However, one benefit it offers, and it's important, is that it is a good starting point for the interview. (In the interview you will learn how frank and complete the resumé is.)

➤ Always have **interviews conducted by two or even three people** each interviewing the applicant either as a group or separately in the first round. Take notes as the interviews proceed and meet afterwards to compare information and impressions and to assess the candidate's suitability for the position. Ask open-ended questions, such as, "What did you enjoy most about your previous position? What least? What was most challenging? What was most boring? Share with me an occasion when you felt like quitting and why. Tell me about a time when you worked extremely long and hard and how you felt about it. Give me an example of a conflict you had with another person, how you handled it and the result. When was the last time you lost your temper at work and why?"

➤ After eliminating the obviously unsuitable candidates, **conduct a second interview.** Confirm previous information. Ask about areas where you and the other interviewers had differing impressions to clarify the reasons for the difference. Ask situational questions relevant to the job to be done, such as, "What did you do in a situation such as…?" or, "How did you handle such a situation?" All questions should be developed to gain information that relates to the requirements of the position. At this point it is important to have the applicant interviewed by the person who will be their supervisor. This person can usually determine if the applicant is technically competent and has the required job skills.

➢ Once you have reduced the number of candidates to between two and five, **conduct background and reference checks** with previous employers and one or two of their references. Reference checks are a challenge, because some employers provide only minimal information such as length of service. Usually the best information is obtained by contacting the person your applicant worked for directly. Tell them the reason you are calling, ask them if they want to call you back so they can be sure of your identity. Ask about duties performed, attendance, work effort etc. Then ask the reference what they would consider to be the applicant's two or three greatest strengths and what area of improvement they would suggest . Of course a "must" question is, "Would you rehire?" You might ask what types of positions the reference thinks would best suit this applicant. What situations do they think the applicant should avoid? Listen very carefully for any indication of negativity and note it for future follow-up.

➢ As part of their background checks some organizations are also doing **credit checks** if this is relevant to the job: and **criminal checks** in situations where children, or seniors could be at risk. Others are verifying **educational achievements and professional designations** because this data is so often falsified on applications and resumes.

Society is becoming increasingly concerned about access to and the privacy of personal information. In response to these issues governments are drafting and enacting legislation to protect individuals and control this type of information. Employers, therefore, are ensuring that applicants are aware and agree that background checks will be done. They do this by inserting a statement on the application form which the applicant is asked to sign. It usually reads something similar to this:

> "The applicant hereby authorizes and grants permission to this organization to inquire about and verify the information which has been provided. The applicant also authorizes previous employers, educational institutions, references or others contacted to provide the requested information and recognizes that this information may influence the hiring decision."

CAUTION

Never contact the applicant's *current* employer without permission. Their employer may not be aware they are searching for a new job and it could jeopardize their continued employment. Never divulge information provided by a previous employer or a reference to the applicant.

➤ Finally, develop or purchase **an appropriate test or assessment** of the applicant's job suitability. There are many available which have been validated. The key concern must be that the test is non-discriminatory and that it measures elements important to actual job success. An assessment tool the authors have used with great success measures the extent to which the applicant possesses personality characteristics such as Diplomatic or Independent, Cooperative or Competitive, Submissive or Assertive, Self-Sufficient or Group Oriented, Reserved or Outgoing. This assessment document also indicates personal aspects such as Abilities, and Motivation and Interests. Interestingly, it may reveal that an applicant scores high in abilities such as Working with Numbers,

Working with Words or Working with Shapes while the Motivation/Interest section indicates little or no interest in one of these areas. Structured assessment tools disclose and define attributes that are almost impossible to determine in an interview. In addition, they measure and reveal extremes in any of the characteristics. These are difficult to recognize or score in any other way.

CAUTION

Never, never, never **make a hiring, transfer or promotion decision** *solely* **on the basis of an assessment document, interview(s), or favorable reference checks. Consider all of the information available from the interviews, resumé, reference checks, personal observation, and assessment results. If there is any doubt continue with further interviews and checks.**

Before using any assessment document it is imperative to ensure that it is non-discriminatory, evaluates factors that are important to job success and has been validated.

Observations

Researchers recently have indicated that up to 90 percent of job performance and organizational success is dependent on assigning people to jobs appropriate to their interests, natural talents, and personality characteristics. It is easier by far to hire people who are already motivated to do what you need done than to try and motivate an unwilling, uninterested, unmotivated individual. A normally favorable characteristic, when too extreme, may be a serious liability in a certain situation or responsibility.

Participate in the best training you can find in job definition, interviewing, selection, and hiring skills. This knowledge will prove invaluable throughout your career. Offer to help others in interviewing applicants. Your time will be well rewarded by the additional experience you gain.

Keep searching until you find an assessment document that you find useful. Then use the document at every opportunity **until you are able to easily relate the assessment report information to observable behaviors** on the job and to their impact on job performance and success.

A FINAL CAUTION – There have been many instances where a teacher, manager or executive has misjudged the abilities of an individual. Examples:

> "You'll never make it. Four groups are out. Go back to Liverpool." - a Decca Records executive to the Beatles in 1962.

> In 1954 Jim Denny, manager of the Grand Ole Opry, fired Elvis Presley after one performance. He suggested to Elvis, "You oughta' go back to drivin' a truck." Of course we know Elvis went on to become one of the most popular singers in America.

> Louis L'Amour wrote over 100 western novels with more than 200 million copies in print. Little known is the fact that he received 350 rejections before his first book was accepted by a publisher.

"Success or failure in any endeavor is caused more by mental attitude than by mental capacities for almost all of us."

- Dr. William Osler, Internationally Renowned Physician and Professor

"When you hire the right person, you can do no wrong. When you hire the wrong person, despite your best efforts, you can do no right."   **– Anonymous**

A Smile Break

Are you suitable for these positions?

"Magician has a position for an attractive young lady to assist in a cutting-off-the-head illusion. Good salary and medical benefits."

"Mixer operator wanted for position in dynamite factory. Some travel, at short notice, may be required."

Because

9

They Think They Have
Something To Gain and Nothing To Lose

Why?

Because

They are inclined to be opportunists. Having observed what happens in the workplace, they have come to believe (rightly or wrongly) that there are few payoffs *for* doing what is expected and, conversely, rarely any penalties *for not* doing what is expected.

What frustrates us more than people who could do what we expect but don't? We know they could do it because they've done it before. We are certain they know what to do, how to do it, that they have the resources, and understand the process and procedures. In spite of this, tasks are partially done, done late, or done incorrectly. Work effort is less than we can reasonably expect. Sometimes they perform to expectations and sometimes they don't. We just can't be certain of what they are likely to do.

A challenging few are in an avoidance mode, thinking of ways to avoid doing what is expected.

They do what they have to do to gain the payoffs. But they look for shortcuts, circumvent rules, or bypass the process to gain the benefits with the least effort possible.

The Linkage: From attitudes to results

Some employees think they're smarter than others in their peer group. In fact they believe they're smarter than the "boss." They've got things "figured out," especially the distinction between what they must do and don't need to do. These beliefs have developed over time by observing what happens in the department and in the overall organization. They are aware of those who have underperformed without negative consequences. Conversely, they know that the best performers in the group receive no additional pay, little recognition, and no praise for their extra effort. **They have come to the conclusion that they might as well do as little as possible and that those who do more are idiots.**

They feel smug, superior, and confident in their analysis of the system. No matter what they do or don't do, they are sure there will be no serious negative consequences. In many cases, they consider it a challenge to beat the system and enjoy doing it. For them it adds excitement and challenge to an otherwise boring job. In this way, they create their own intangible rewards.

Some want to do nothing. They like to play "catch me if you can." In a few extreme cases they develop elaborate and complex schemes to avoid effort of any kind (they work at plotting how not to work). They find places to hide and take time to preplan excuses.

A few take the opposite approach: they want to reap whatever benefits are available, but do as little as possible to earn them. They calculate how they can maximize rewards with devious methods and strategies. The extreme cases are, for example, those few corporate CEOs with attractive stock option and bonus plans who have been extremely innovative in their use of questionable accounting methods that maximize their payouts. A number have been persuasive and powerful enough to convince their accounting firms to collaborate with their schemes to the detriment of shareholders. According to reports in the business press, accounting and legal firms have, in some cases, initiated these questionable tactics.

The results are generally predictable. When such unacceptable behaviors are ignored and allowed to continue without negative consequences, others in the workgroup or industry follow the same path. Over a period of time there is a drift in this direction and other groups adopt similar behaviors. In extreme cases, even large organizations are totally overtaken by such behavior and they become the norms in a corporate culture of minimal effort and unproductive behaviors.

BIG BILL

This was Jim's first day as a supervisor in the department and of course he was both nervous and excited. Much of the day was spent in meeting the employees, reviewing the production schedule, checking on past reports, and verifying the day's output. Towards the end of the shift he realized that one of the workers never seemed to be doing anything.

"What does that fellow do?" he asked one of the other employees. The employee told him that the person's name was Bill and he did nothing but sit and read pocket books.

"Why is that?" Jim asked.

"We don't know, he's been here for almost four months and has never done anything but read. We think the previous supervisor was afraid of him and didn't know what to do with him."

Jim could understand why the prior supervisor might have been intimidated. Bill weighed more than 300 pounds and stood over six feet tall. With long hair, a bushy beard and wearing the leathers of a biker, he was an imposing and intimidating figure. Frankly, Jim didn't know what to do either. Since the day was almost over, he let it go. Overnight he couldn't sleep, just tossing and turning. In the morning he still hadn't come up with a solution.

Once he reached the plant he went directly to Bill and said, "Bill I've just started as you know. What is it you're supposed to be working at here?"

"Darned if I know," Bill responded easily. "No one has ever told me what to do. Give me something to do and I'll do it and do it well."

Jim found him a job manning a tool crib and Bill did it well, as promised. Problem solved. There was no incentive for Bill to do something and no penalty for doing nothing, so he did nothing and waited to see if anyone would ever give him work to do.

If you doubt that this kind of thing can happen, a friend reading a draft copy of this information shared with us the fact that she was once hired as a Project Manager and assigned no duties for six months. This occurred in spite of her repeated requests to her manager (who traveled frequently) and to other leaders in the organization.

INCENTIVES BACKFIRE – HERMAN HAS TO GO

Herman was not a likeable guy. As Plant Manager in a unit of over 270 employees, he was what most people would call a "bull in a china shop," or a "hard-nosed SOB." Those who worked for him tolerated him at best. He trusted few, was suspicious of the rest, and could not seem to keep from being dictatorial and disparaging. It was his natural inclination. To his credit, he was loyal to the company, tried hard to improve productivity, and attempted to improve his leadership techniques. But regardless of what he tried, things didn't click.

Some might say it was because his heart wasn't in it. Others would say it was because he didn't have a heart.

He had a wide variety of employees, from skilled machinists and electricians to assemblers, forklift drivers, and cleanup people. The problem was that the plant was not as productive as the General Manager expected. Frankly, it was not as productive as Herman wanted either. In desperation, Herman had tried everything he could think of: praise, threats, time studies, employee involvement meetings, and other team approaches. Nothing moved the numbers to where he felt they should have been. Finally, Herman remembered an incentive program that seemed to have worked at another plant. It was a time-off program that allowed employees not to go home but to go to the cafeteria when their work targets for the day had been met.

When Herman suggested the program, the union was opposed. Human Resources was also against it, but the General Manager, although dubious, finally approved it. A rumble of complaints began within a few days. About one third of the people were finishing early each day, some finished 30 minutes early and others as much as 90 minutes early. But there were those in the plant, such as the machinist operators, who couldn't finish sooner because their machine speeds were preset and couldn't be increased. There was no possible way for them to leave early. Forklift drivers were in a similar situation because they had to be available to the end of the shift. In fact, anyone servicing others could not leave until everyone in that area had finished.

Too late, Herman realized that while one-third of his people were happy with the new program, the other two-thirds felt cheated and began a work-to-rule campaign. They went through the motions but achieved less. The hostility forced Herman to revert to the former work arrangements.

He could have avoided this situation if he had taken the time to talk to a few of the people in each of the trades to identify potential problems. But then Herman wouldn't have been Herman. He "lost face" and shortly after the General Manager took pity and transferred him to another plant. To his chagrin, Herman learned that ill-conceived incentive programs can be explosive, double edged, and career damaging.

The manager who replaced Herman, spent his first week talking to every employee. He asked for complaints, problems and suggestions. He listened carefully and developed a list. Then he asked several of the informal group leaders if they would help him "fix things." Using this group approach, and with assistance from process engineering, they redesigned the workflow. At the same time they addressed employee complaints and incorporated some of their best ideas into the new scheme. Problem solved. Productivity improved. Herman gone.

When and why does this type of problem occur?

Sometimes when a new manager is appointed, one or more individuals test the manager to determine if the new boss knows what should be happening and the results that should be achieved. Next they set out to learn what this person will tolerate. They either test the limits themselves or encourage someone else to do the testing, while they observe safely from the sidelines.

Occasionally these problems occur because the manager unconsciously and unintentionally rewards undesirable behaviors. A specific outcome is expected but the employee sees a reward in doing otherwise.

This problem may also creep into an organization over a period of time. Individuals such as these begin to realize that the manager is distracted by other concerns, tired of the effort involved in running his area. In some cases, the manager adopts the same behaviors as his problem people (for many of the same reasons).

Those in authority are either not aware of what is happening or they are ignoring the problem. Therefore people aren't held accountable for their behaviors or results. If this continues, gradually the problem grows. More people follow the same path. The seriousness of the deficiencies becomes greater and more frequent. Other factors may be that the manager doesn't know how to set expectations or is reluctant to ask. He or she may not know how to use corrective discipline or may feel that the organization will not support such action if it is taken.

The problem grows to such an extent that it cannot be ignored and someone in greater authority steps in and replaces the manager with someone who can and will correct matters. Another factor that creates these problems is a lack of rewards or recognition for great effort and work well done. The omission causes people to feel undervalued so they decide to do less and care less.

Variations of this problem

More frequently than normal or than expected those who think they have something to gain and nothing to lose avoid responsibility and accountability. They maximize their tardy arrival, lunch time and break times, and call in sick when in fact they're not ill.

Some engage in minor theft and pilferage (such as padding expense accounts, or taking home small items) or utilize company equipment and facilities for personal use (such as telephones, computers, copying machines and vehicles).

Those looking for something to gain may deliberately restrict their effort and output to justify overtime premium pay. Those who think they've got nothing to lose will "goof around" and play pranks on others to kill time.

A few go to the extreme of finding secluded places where they can nap or read without detection.

Fixing it and preventing it in future

When some individuals feel they have nothing to lose and something to gain, the situation can be corrected **by making them understand that they do have something to lose when they don't meet expectations:**

➤ Usually the best way to begin is to **talk** to the person alone, advise them that their negative behavior or unsatisfactory performance has been observed and give them recent examples.

➤ Ask for an **explanation**. Obtain their commitment that the problem will cease.

➤ If it is serious or there have been previous problems, **caution them** that the next time this happens there will be negative consequences in terms of corrective action.

➤ Before ending the conversation, ask if they understand that you are serious and ask them if you can count on their cooperation. **Get their verbal commitment**.

➤ Then closely **monitor** their behavior.

➤ If they return to their former behavior, take the appropriate, corrective **disciplinary action**. Conversely, if they maintain their favorable behavior take the time to acknowledge the improvement.

Keep in mind that both payoffs and penalties already exist in most companies. Great care must be exercised in introducing any change to ensure that the desired results will be achieved and negative possibilities have been considered and eliminated.

CAUTION
Always **do what you say you are going to do.** *Never* **promise or threaten what you can't deliver. If you don't, you lose credibility, trust and respect. You create your reputation and once created it's difficult to change.**

To prevent these problems:

> ➤ **Be aware of what is happening or not happening** in your area and take prompt and appropriate action.
> ➤ This **attention should be focused on both reliable**, conscientious employees and those less reliable.
> ➤ **Positive feedback for productive performers reinforces such behavior** and therefore it continues and grows. Lack of positive reinforcement usually results, over time, in a decline in performance by these reliable people.

In the case of schemers and opportunists, lack of management attention is seen as a circumstance to be exploited. They'll use it to their very best advantage and usually to management's detriment. But if the manager is alert and takes prompt action, they realize it and curb their actions. In short order, each supervisor and manager knows which employees require more attention. These people are sometimes referred to as high-maintenance employees.

Once these opportunists become convinced that their manager is *always aware* of what's happening *and will act accordingly* they begin to curtail their negative tendencies. Since they are usually capable and intelligent they can become excellent performers.

Observations

Payoffs and penalties will not solve systemic problems. They are effective only for behaviors and results totally within the control and capability of the individual.

Some managers introduce incentive programs to "bribe" employees to do what they are already paid to do. They do this because they are unable or unwilling to clearly communicate expectations and to use appropriate and available disciplinary measures. Incentives are usually not as effective as rewards.

Take great care prior to introducing reward programs. Ensure that everyone will be able to benefit proportionately, that the payoffs are equitable, that the methods of measuring and accounting for performance are easily determined, transparent and understood. Finally, consider future situations such as recessions, organizational changes and other relevant factors and what the impact they may have on the program and its methods.

Clearly state that the program will be reviewed annually and may be altered as conditions change. Reward programs based on the achievement of predetermined individual, departmental and organizational goals that are specific, reviewed quarterly and reset annually are usually the most relevant and effective.

When you observe negative behavior ask yourself what the person expects to gain by his or her actions. Whether conscious or unconscious, their actions (what they do and *don't* do) are governed by a desire to achieve some gain or avoid some possible effort or loss.

> *"We cannot change character but we can change behavior through incentives and penalties."*
> **– Alan Greenspan, Chairman U S Federal Reserve**

A Smile Break

> *"Hard work pays off in the future, laziness pays off now."*
> **– Zen Thoughts**

Another Smile Break

Excuses for sleeping on the job:

> ➢ "I read that napping is one of the habits of highly successful people."
> ➢ "The folks at the blood bank told me this could happen."
> ➢ "I wasn't napping on the job; I was meditating on our Vision and Mission Statements."

Because

10

They Are

Disillusioned and Demotivated

Why?

Because

The workplace is dirty, disorganized and unsafe. Needed equipment, materials, and information are not available. There are no up-to-date job instructions, the boss's instructions are always changing. No one trains anyone. Pay and benefits are not competitive. Overtime, pay increases and promotions are decided unfairly. Employees and management treat each other without respect or trust.

In the Getting Started section of this book it was pointed out that early chapters cover problems that are most prevalent and easiest to correct. Later chapters consider problems that are less prevalent but more difficult to solve. This chapter begins the transition.

Here we look at what occurs when managers fail to address most of the issues we've raised so far in this book: a "sick" workplace culture caught in a downward spiral of declining morale and diminishing returns. It seems as if no one in management cares about the employees, or what's happening and not happening. **Worst of all, the employees who truly care feel there is no hope of improvement in the situation.**

Negative conditions and culture are usually the end result of management practices over many years. These practices, behaviors, methods and management style stem from the CEO's attitudes and beliefs about people and what is required to be successful in a competitive business environment.

If the CEO believes that, to compete, the company must keep its payroll and benefit costs lower than its competitors, that training is an unnecessary cost, and that maintaining a clean, organized, safe workplace is a waste of effort and funds, then naturally this is what is done or not done.

The CEO or manager unwittingly creates the negative employee attitudes and culture that he or she dislikes and deplores. Management's perceptions become self-fulfilling prophecies.

The Linkage: From attitudes to results

These employees have come to believe that a job is a job: you can't expect much from management, just do what you have to do; the situation is unlikely to improve, so put up with it.

They feel disappointed and disinterested in what's happening or not happening. They feel the situation is hopeless and unlikely to change. No one in management truly cares.

They generally do what they have to do. They leave promptly at quitting time and demonstrate little interest in how the work unit is performing or its future plans. We might say they are uncommitted, to the job, the manager, or the organization. Their concerns are about their rights and getting everything that's coming to them. On the surface, they seem passive, accepting, even friendly, but they are not emotionally engaged by what's going on.

As a result, performance levels stay at the mandated minimum level. There are few improvement initiatives. Cooperation and support are limited. No one's heart is in what they do. In some cases conditions are appalling but no one moves to improve them. Negative behaviors are prevalent but management takes no corrective action. Eventually productivity declines and profits follow suit.

FLYING CHICKEN INNARDS

Normally I don't pick up hitchhikers. But this guy walking down the road near a chicken-processing factory looked tired and dejected. Maybe that's what prompted me to stop. I asked where he was going.

"Home," he said. He didn't offer any more information.

"What are you doing heading into town at this time of day?" I asked.

"I just quit my job," he responded. "It finally got to me. Today the people on the line were throwing chicken guts at each other again. It's dangerous, it's messy, and it's a waste. But the supervisor won't do anything about it and neither will the plant manager. I think I can do better somewhere else," he sighed.

In negative circumstances good, hardworking employees tend to leave. In this case, the company lost a dedicated, conscientious employee by its inability or unwillingness to provide a safe working environment.

CHRIS, COLLEGE AND COMPUTERS

Chris was a pretty happy camper. Due to start a college computer science course in the fall, he had just landed a part-time job with a small computer sales and repair retailer. Unfortunately, he quickly learned that the place was a shambles. Inventory was stacked haphazardly in any nook and cranny. The inventory records were totally out of date and useless. Being conscientious and anxious to learn he talked to the owner and offered to straighten the place out, even volunteered to do it on his own time. The following week he did just that and when he left that night the place was neat and orderly. He was proud of what he had accomplished. Pride turned to disgust when he reported for work the following week and found the premises and stock in the same condition as before. He left soon after.

The owner demonstrated a lack of concern for organization, an inability to maintain orderliness, and a lack of appreciation for what Chris had done. He lost a conscientious employee who was willing to do more than expected.

THE HOT WATER TAP—AND THE DRIP

It was an Engineering Department of about 35 people with Doug Jamieson as the Chief Engineer. The General Manager was a supporter and promoter of participative leadership methods. He convinced Doug that such methods were the "thing to do" and that they would generate important benefits. Human Resources met with Doug on several occasions to provide insights, describe the approaches, develop a plan of action and generally prepare Doug for the initial meeting with his staff. The Human Resources specialist was careful to caution Doug that sometimes people in a department will bring up a minor complaint to gauge the reaction and commitment of the manager. If this happened he was told to acknowledge it and promise speedy action to rectify it.

Launch day came. The employees were all in attendance. Doug introduced the principles, methods, and benefits. Then he asked if there were any particular things the group would like to begin working to improve.

"Could we start with something easy," one brave soul inquired, "and get the hot water tap in the men's washroom fixed? It's given us nothing but cold water for the last three years."

Doug grew flustered and responded, "We're not here for piddly things like that, has anyone got anything else?"

There were no further suggestions, the meeting concluded, and the participative leadership initiative died.

Doug had given the employees the answer they were looking for. Nothing was really going to change because Doug was unable or unwilling to change his leadership style.

When and why does this type of problem occur?

Employees become demotivated and disillusioned when they believe that management cares little about people, is tolerant of negative behavior, unconcerned about proper working conditions, and not committed to effective performance.

The conditions, climate and culture in the company decline and become increasingly negative and management seems to be doing nothing to improve them. One of the reasons may be that the manager has been in the situation for so long and the decline has been so gradual that he or she simply doesn't realize how severe and unacceptable it has become. Other factors may be that the manager is distant, uninvolved, self-absorbed or focused on other aspects of his/her responsibilities. In some cases the manager's natural talents are in the technical or financial areas necessary to his position, but he or she lacks the people and organizational skills.

Finally, some managers realize what has happened but don't know how to improve it and won't seek help either from inside or outside the organization. They think that to do so would be a sign of weakness or they don't want others (head office, the Human Resources department) to become aware of the situation.

Variations of this problem

People lose motivation when there is no discipline: When employees can "goof off" or harass others and no corrective action is taken.

They grow disillusioned when there is a great deal of criticism and little, if any, praise, appreciation or recognition. They feel the same when their ideas and suggestions are ignored and discouraged or when promises are sometimes made, but seldom kept.

When management doesn't communicate any sense of mission, vision, goals, or priorities, or any indication of how the department or company is performing, employees feel they are being kept "in the dark" deliberately.

Fixing it and preventing it in future

Once this state of malaise has been reached, it is extremely difficult for the CEO/manager personally to bring about changes to correct conditions. The CEO/owner/manager who leads the organization has these options:

1. **Change his/her methods** and practices (difficult to accept and to do).
2. **Recruit external consulting resources** to assist in these efforts (can be effective if the CEO will allow and support change).
3. **Step aside** and turn over leadership responsibilities to a person who has the required skills and experience (and then personally support their initiatives).

Large organizations that recognize the difficulty in getting leaders to change their methods usually reassign them, providing everyone an opportunity to "start over." They may terminate them or appoint them to an "advisory" position at another location. Increasingly they arrange for mentoring by an external resource person.

For the rare CEO/manager who recognizes and accepts the need to change his/her methods there is hope and help. This book details many improvement methods. However, the CEO/manager will need to identify **someone (either inside or outside the company) who has the necessary capabilities and qualities to assist**. Qualities they will require are the ability, courage and perseverance to bluntly say, "There's a better way. Here's why and here's what has to be done differently. Here's how we're going to do it and how we will measure progress." **Start sooner rather than later**. Suppress a natural inclination to grouse about the cost. Observe and learn from this person.

Preventing this type of problem begins with developing **a clear understanding/picture/idea** of what method and practices lead to a positive culture and motivated work force. This can be done by reading, visiting other companies, attending courses and conferences and talking to people outside your organization who you trust and respect.

As managers we must be aware of difficulties, find solutions and do so promptly. **There are always some dedicated employees who want to and will contribute to improvements provided they are given the encouragement, resources, and approvals by management.** However, when they repeatedly experience delays, obstacles, and barriers that they feel are solvable by management, they eventually give up in frustration. Consider the following in your appeal to those who are willing to help:

> ➤ The easiest, fastest and most effective way of re-enlisting their commitment is to **ask them what three things they feel management should tackle** in order to improve conditions. Another is to use an employee survey. The results will identify the priorities. Then select the most important and begin working on solutions.

➤ Projects that interest them will motivate them. Assign some **action items** to individuals, some to managers and some to problem-solving teams.
➤ Regularly **communicate progress** and completion.
➤ Give appropriate **recognition** for achievements. Employees begin to adopt a more motivated attitude after a series of positive experiences.

Observations

The decline and ultimate failure of any organization, whether it is an agency, a business, a service club or even a country, usually begins imperceptibly. Things are allowed to slip, expectations are lowered, unacceptable behaviors and performance are tolerated.
Left to themselves, situations naturally go from bad to worse.

If it is not too late, a new leader reverses the trend and the organization survives and prospers.

When asking employees what needs to be improved, whether in person, or by survey, be prepared for negative feedback and be ready and willing to take prompt action. If not, don't ask, don't start.

On occasion, employees will begin with a minor complaint or suggestion to "test" management's commitment or to determine if it's safe to complain. It is imperative to take seemingly insignificant, issues seriously and act promptly.

To bring about a change in employee motivation, we always have to make changes in the way we lead. These changes must be triggered by a change in the way we think about employees. We need to develop a new mindset.

You can buy people's time and attendance but you cannot buy their enthusiasm, trust, respect or loyalty. You cannot buy their minds, hearts and souls. You have to earn these.
– Anonymous

"It's not the strongest of the species that survive, nor the most intelligent, but the one most responsive to change."
– Charles Darwin

"We've learned that to ignore the facts does not change the facts."
- Anonymous

A Smile Break

> "My formula for success is rise early, work late, and strike oil."
> — J. Paul Getty

Because

11

They Have Significant
Personal
Problems

Why?

Because

Of severe physical or mental illnesses, relationship difficulties or social conditions which may have been present but not evident when hired. They may have developed and worsened over a period of months or years and only now have reached the stage where they are creating a serious performance problem.

The vast majority of employees have had, or will have personal difficulties. It's a normal part of life. Most are able to cope with their problems, resolve the situation and continue to perform well. They carry on with their duties without any apparent negative impact on their behavior or performance. However, for a lesser number, the story is not as simple. The condition is such that it overwhelms them and they struggle to cope with the situation and continue to meet expectations.

Factors that influence the impact on performance include such elements as: the complexity, severity and duration of the condition; the individual's ability to cope; the social support network they can access; the availability and affordability of professional care; their ability and willingness to seek assistance.

Those employees whose performance suffers have usually performed their duties satisfactorily in the past and therefore we know these people have the abilities required. They may fail to meet expectations when they experience one or more of the following: severe emotional distress, mental problems, physical illness, addictions, financial stresses or relationship conflicts.

Avoid judging or stereotyping those who fall into this category. They are not "bad" people. They are simply folks experiencing extreme difficulty. They may be from any walk of life, any level in the firm, any age group, and any ethnic group. There are many famous people who have experienced one or more of these problems. Frank W. Woolworth, the founder of the *F.W. Woolworth* stores for example, twice in his lifetime experienced long bouts of depression, once at a time when he had 500 stores in operation and later in life, when he had more than 1500 stores. After each bout, he returned and continued to expand the business. Mike Wallace of *60 Minutes* television fame has admitted to experiencing three serious bouts of depression. Former U.S. President Gerald Ford's wife Betty battled with addiction. History has shown that many famous artists, writers, and composers have been plagued by a variety of mental disorders. Our daily news media regularly report the cocaine and heroin addictions of actors, sports celebrities, and others.

The Linkage: From attitudes to results

Most people in the above categories are reluctant to reveal their problem(s). Whether it's a physical or a mental illness, they believe that admitting to a difficulty could jeopardize their job security or promotability and affect the way in which they are viewed by management, co-workers, and others. They think they can do their work well enough to escape detection and see no alternative but to struggle on as best they can.

The feelings they experience range from anxiety at the possibility of being detected, confusion in coping with the increasingly difficult situation, insecurity about the job and relationships, fear about what may come next, and feelings of embarrassment and helplessness about what to do and who to trust.

Those with health problems naturally are concerned about their mortality, the cost of medical treatment, and the future welfare of those they care most about.

Generally they attempt to do their work to the best of their ability because they are dependent on the income. However, because of their particular illness, whether physical or psychological, they will usually experience some difficulty. It may be that they are confused, unable to concentrate, distracted and troubled. They may struggle to maintain the quality, volume, or timeliness of their output. There may be emotional outbursts in which anger and hostility drive them to physical or verbal attacks on co-workers, customers, or suppliers. They may isolate themselves, avoiding normal situations, certain responsibilities, or certain people. At times, during the day, they may inexplicably disappear from their workplace. There is a greater frequency of absenteeism among troubled workers. This absenteeism may follow a pattern; it may always occur on Fridays and/or Mondays or on three or four consecutive days each month. They tend to experience medical problems more frequently than most because of their basic underlying problems. There may be observable signs of illness or addiction such as unsteadiness when they walk, the smell of alcohol or marijuana on their breath (or mouthwash, garlic or some other substance they use to mask the odor).

These serious problems usually result in absenteeism, errors, responsibilities avoided, reduced productivity, and strained relationships or confrontations with fellow employees or the manager.

WHEN WORK IS A REFUGE

Grant knew he had a difficult performance review to conduct. He felt that he had prepared himself thoroughly to talk to Frank about his memory lapses, the consequences and the possibility of Frank's early retirement. When it was over it seemed to him that the interview had gone well. They had discussed various projects and performance elements and then, gently, Grant had introduced the observation that Frank seemed to be losing his memory, even with simple day-to-day assignments.

"Frank you've put in over 36 years," he said in a friendly way. "Why don't you think about taking early retirement in a few months when you're 63, or sooner if you want to?"

Frank had nodded and promised to think about it.

That weekend, without warning or saying a word, Frank purchased a hose, drove to a remote location, connected the hose to the exhaust pipe of the car, and asphyxiated himself. Only later was management able to piece together the details of why it happened. What they learned was that a long miserable marriage, plus the onslaught of Alzheimer's disease, capped by the suggestion of early retirement, triggered the suicide. Frank felt the job was his rock and his refuge. There seemed no other reason to live.

This terrible and sad outcome may have been prevented by earlier action. Once signs of memory lapses and performance difficulties were obvious, Grant should have had a discussion with Frank to attempt to uncover the reasons and discuss possible options including a visit to his physician.

Never allow concerns to accumulate and then attempt to resolve them all during the annual performance review. Deal with issues as they arise, one by one.

THE INSIDIOUS ENEMY INSIDE

Sometimes, rumors are the precursors to facts. Rumor had it that Michael was in some kind of difficulty. His walk was unsteady, his speech somewhat slurred, and he acted as though he was weak and tired. It seemed to be getting worse. However, when asked if he had a problem or needed help he shrugged off the questions. Twenty-six years with the company, nine of them in management, Michael was a solid, respected manager and a man who prized his independence.

Although others tried to cover up what was happening, eventually one of his employees cautiously and reluctantly approached Human Resources about the situation. The only reason he did it was because of his concern for Michael's safety. Michael was continuing to drive and often walked through the plant and around the property putting himself at risk of injury. It required three meetings with Human Resources before Michael would agree to a physical examination by the company physician. The diagnosis was Lou Gerhig's disease. Its symptoms are a gradual deterioration in muscle strength throughout the whole body and there is no known cure. The challenge was that Michael's mind was fine and his thought processes intact and he wanted to continue to work for a period of time. He was able to continue to work because his duties were changed and the workplace was modified to allow for his limitations. Delicately and with great sensitivity, the Human Resources Manager, Michael's manager, and Michael's wife finally convinced him that continuation was not a viable option due to the progress of the illness.

HEAR, SEE, DO AND SPEAK NO EVIL

This particular company had four people at one location who were all in difficulty because of alcohol.

Dave was at the executive level as Director of Procurement and Logistics. Those in his department and other executives knew his secret. A bottle of Scotch kept in the glove compartment of his company car parked in the executive garage, which he visited at least twice each day on one pretense or another. To cover the smell of alcohol on his breath, he would chew a small piece of garlic or chewing gum. The General Manager, Dave's direct report, reluctantly persuaded Dave to seek assistance.

Dave finally sought help, spent a month in a rehabilitation facility but returned to his addiction. While this relapse obviously was Dave's personal responsibility, the General Manager was partially to blame because he didn't maintain the pressure to reform and do it consistently and persistently. Finally, he encouraged Dave to accept an early retirement package. Dave died several years later, still addicted.

Ron was a manager in the Human Resources Department. His daily alcohol intake began during breakfast. This was sufficient until noon when he regularly visited a nearby restaurant for lunch. Lunch usually consisted of a half-eaten sandwich and three double white rums with water. No effort was made to mask the odor of alcohol since it was consumed off site. Ron reported to the Director of Human Resources who avoided the issue by saying the addiction didn't affect Ron's job performance ignoring the fact that Ron was setting an example completely inappropriate to his position. Ron never sought treatment, retired early, and also died an addict.

What Dave and Ron had in common was not only their addiction to alcohol, but the fact that they were mean and manipulative in their interactions with others in their peer group and to subordinates. This aspect of their behavior was unknown to the General Manager. He chose to ignore the known drinking problem because the two men seemed to be performing adequately.

Jack Menzies was a supervisor in Production Planning. Again, those in the area and in related departments knew he had a problem with alcohol. No one in a position of authority was willing to confront Jack and bring about change until Larry Wilson was appointed manager of the department. At the first sign of an alcohol-related problem, he immediately called Jack into his office and calmly told Jack that his problem was well known. He gave him examples and told him that from that point on, these behaviors and performance lapses would not be tolerated.

Larry said, "Jack you now have two choices: you can continue with your drinking and I will have to use corrective disciplinary procedures or you can finally get the help you need through our Employee Assistance Program. Which will it be? Think about it overnight and we'll talk about it again tomorrow."

Next day, Jack said he wanted help and would begin the tough process of kicking his habit. Over the next few weeks, he received counseling and joined Alcoholics Anonymous. Two months later, Mrs. Menzies called Larry.

"Mr. Wilson," she said. "Jack has told me about the ultimatum you gave him and I called to thank you for what you have done. You've not only changed Jack, you've changed our financial situation and we are finally becoming a true family again. You've given us back a husband and a father. I can never thank you enough."

Larry saved a person's life just as surely as a fireman who pulls someone from a burning building.

Then there was Scotty Ferguson. Three times he was fired from his job in the plant for consuming alcohol on company premises. Three times the union, as a final demand in its contract negotiations, insisted on his return. Scotty was a likeable guy who had never lost his Scottish accent or dry Celtic sense of humor. Despite stays in rehabilitation, warnings from management and the firings, he could not shake his dependency on alcohol. One week back at work and he was found passed out on the floor of a washroom stall, lying in a pool of vomit.

"Leave me alone," he told those who drove him home to his sparse and dingy apartment. "Stop bringing me back. I know drinking is going to kill me and I don't care."

These were Scotty's last words to his colleagues. He was found dead four months later.

What is interesting in this example is the way in which each situation was handled. While Dave, Ron, and Scotty's drinking problems were allowed to continue for a long period of time. Larry was helped because his new boss confronted the issue as soon as it became apparent.

When and why does this type of problem occur?

Researchers and scientists are making giant advances in learning the causes of both physical and mental illnesses. However, what they have learned is just the tip of the iceberg. There are myriad causes for these problems. They could be genetic, environmental, or learned behaviors. Analyzing specific causes is best left to professionals trained and experienced in this field.

Variations of this problem

Significant personal problems tend to fall under these five major headings:

➤ **Physical Health Problems** – which could range from cancer and heart disease, to strokes or any one of many other diseases.

➤ **Emotional Problems** – such as chronic depression, manic depression, or obsessive-compulsive behaviors or other forms of mental disorders.

➢ **Addiction Problems** – in which the person is addicted to alcohol, prescription drugs, illegal drugs, gambling, pornography, or a combination of these.

➢ **Financial Problems** – which may be the result of unfortunate spending habits or investment decisions or the result of a costly addiction which leads to excessive debt, increased desperation and, in some extreme cases, criminal acts to obtain the funds required.

➢ **Family Problems** – which may center on a child, a spouse, or eldercare situation or be the result of one of the problems listed above.

An employee may appear to have a relationship problem, but the root cause is often one or more of the above factors. It is common for some people to have an interwoven cluster of problems. For example, when there is an alcohol, drug or gambling problem, there is usually a financial problem because of the costs involved. If the individual is married, there often is a family problem because of the other two.

Instances of erratic behavior may seem human or even innocent enough when they happen. But we have to be aware of the deep and complicated issues that may be behind them. The question is, how do you handle those issues?

Fixing it and preventing it in future

First, don't be overwhelmed by the complexity and severity of these situations or by the volume of information provided here. Continue reading and you will see that your role and responsibility in these cases is much different than those in previous chapters. Your challenge is to be a **necessary and positive catalyst** for treatment and resolution.

Physical and mental illnesses are treatable, but not always curable. Neither are they considered a problem unless and until they negatively affect behavior or performance or pose a danger to the individual or to others.

Avoid the temptation to act the part of psychologist or psychiatrist. Be an attentive listener but don't pry into their lives.

Many of the famous as well as those in the general population are able to work and perform extremely well once they have received treatment.

CAUTION
Never attempt to diagnose the problem or accuse or counsel the employee. Simply present them with the facts of the situation. Inappropriate advice could worsen the situation. Assistance is always better left to professionals who are trained and experienced in this field.

Your role and responsibility is to convince those with personal difficulties to seek and utilize professional assistance and to do this in a sensitive but firm manner. The task begins with being aware of behaviors and performance deficiencies that are worsening and are unacceptable. Before meeting with the person you should:

➤ **Record the details** of date, time, location, situation, and behavior or performance deficiency.
➤ **Learn your organization's policies, procedures, past practices and rules** for dealing with this type of situation. For example, in the case of an alcohol problem, do company rules prohibit possession or consumption or is it being under the influence of alcohol on company property? In the case of a verbal or physical assault, what are the rules and procedures?
➤ **Obtain advice** on a step-by-step plan for a discussion with the person. Usually someone from Human Resources will personally assist you in preparing for, and may be present at, discussions with the employee.

➤ **Think about possible reactions** such as denial and excuses and prepare yourself to respond appropriately. If possible, role-play the situation with the Human Resources specialist to ensure you are prepared.

➤ **Select a private office** where you can meet with the person unobserved and a time when few others are in the area. Be sensitive to the discomfort the employee will feel.

Begin your conversation in a calm, friendly manner, perhaps with a question. Here are some examples of the right approach:

"Mary, thank you for taking this time to meet with me."

"You may or may not realize it, but I've been concerned about you."

"How have you been feeling lately"?

"Is anything bothering you? The reason I ask is because of some things that I've noticed recently."

"You seem more upset than usual."

"The other day, you criticized Carl and lost your temper. It seems to be happening more often and becoming more serious. Your job performance is slipping as well. Can you tell me what's happening?"

Show that you are listening to their answers. Nod to encourage more information. Do not interrupt. When the person stops ask, "Is there anything else you feel is important or want to share with me?"

If the person denies there is a problem, it is not unusual. Addicts typically deny they have a problem and tend to be well prepared with all types of excuses.

State that these behaviors cannot be overlooked and advise the employee that there is help available to them. At this point inform them of the company's Employee Assistance Program or appropriate community resources. Explain their purpose, how they function, the fact that the services are confidential and outline the steps they need to take to access this support.

It is important at this point to insist on the employee's decision that they will take the next step and contact the resource center or that they are going to attempt improvement without assistance. Advise them again that you are concerned and supportive but that the behaviors and unsatisfactory performance cannot continue. Tell them that you will be looking for improvement and that, without it, progressive corrective discipline will be your only recourse.

Some employees will only admit to a problem once progressive discipline has reached the point where they are about to lose their job. Only then, possibly, they may admit to a problem and ask for assistance. In anticipation of this tendency, it might be relevant to say, "You know my expectations, if for any reason you feel you cannot meet them, come and talk to me before the situation gets worse."

In situations where the employee has no control of the problem such as physical illness, advise the employee of the company medical benefits and any provision for long term disability. Explore potential reassignment to duties which the employee can perform.

The manager who supervises the addict is in the position of having the most powerful influence on bringing about change. "Authority to terminate" is the leverage, which can convince the individual to seek assistance. Be consistent and unrelenting in its use. The situation requires a balance of firmness and sensitivity. It's what has become known as "tough love" in an organizational setting: the manager has to keep demonstrating care and concern while insisting that expectations be met.

Similarly the manager can help employees with financial or relationship concerns, not by providing personal advice, but by providing information on company benefit plans and services and on counselling services available in the community.

As mentioned earlier, these types of physical or psychological problems can occur at any stage in life. When existing employees develop a problem our challenge and responsibility is to get them to utilize effective professional treatment.

From a preventative standpoint, the best we can do is to avoid hiring those with problems so serious that they will be unable to perform to expectations. This can usually be done in the selection and assessment process. Skilled interviewers can often identify those with such problems during the interview and verify their concerns in their background and reference checks.

Always be careful of those who have had frequent job changes and be aware that the applicant may not have listed all of the positions they have held.

Many people with mental or physical challenges can be valuable employees when in appropriate positions – that suit what they "can do" and do not require them to attempt what they "can't do." Within the last decade employers have made great strides in hiring those previously considered unemployable. As a result they have gained employees who, when properly placed, perform conscientiously, with a pleasing spirit of service and great loyalty.

CAUTION
Never begin by accusing someone of having a problem.
You could be wrong. Begin by discussing the observable
behaviors and performance deficiencies.

Observations

Looking back at our story of "Hear, See, Do and Speak No Evil," it is not particularly unusual to find so many individuals with alcohol problems in one company. Addiction research has determined that one person in ten to one in thirteen in North America has a drinking problem.

Some cannot be helped despite our best efforts but the trying is what makes us caring managers and the world a kinder place. It also builds respect with others who are aware of our efforts and the organization's support.

The individual acting on his or her own can seldom cure an addiction. Habits can be overcome this way, but addictions can't. Professional assistance is usually required.

The individual usually will not seek this help unless forced to do so by the threat of losing their job. Potential job loss is a strong motivator because the job provides the money necessary to feed their habit. An addict will often risk losing family before risking the loss of employment.

> *"Most work and professional difficulties arise from emotional and personality problems, not from technical ineptitude or technological change. Emotional issues are the single greatest cause of absenteeism, especially if the physical symptoms of emotional problems are included."*
> **– David W. Krueger, M.D., author of** *Emotional Business*

> *"It is one of the most beautiful compensations in this life that no man can sincerely try to help another without helping himself."*   **– Ralph Waldo Emerson**

A Smile Break

> *"Age does not always bring wisdom. Sometimes age comes alone."*

Another Smile Break

> *"You've got to help me doc,"* the patient pleaded. *"I'm suffering from amnesia, what should I do?"*
> *"Go home and forget about it,"* the doctor replied.

Because

12

They Are

Deliberately Disruptive, Destructive, Unethical or Dangerous

Why?

Because

A few in the work force have developed a deep distrust of authority figures. In extreme cases, this goes beyond distrust to anger or hate. In some cases these feelings are the result of emotional and physical abuse in childhood. Others suffer from undetected learning disabilities that have caused them to suffer low self esteem and unwarranted persecution. In the most rare and extreme situations the person has a severe mental problem or is criminally insane.

In any workplace, you'll encounter a wide spectrum of personalities. Few and far between are the individuals who suffer from some form of clinical psychopathic condition. It's rather like the population of a city. You meet all kinds, but a tiny minority can do damage that far exceeds their numbers.

The Linkage: From attitudes to results

Disruptive employees usually believe those in a position of authority are dishonest, exploitive and uncaring. They think that management deliberately ignores the conditions and situations in which people work and do as little as possible for the workers because they simply can't be bothered, don't care or are only interested in maximizing profits.

A few in this category harbor a pervasive distrust of people in authority. "The boss makes life tough for us," they say, "let's make things tough for him." Some express these sentiments through a mischievous streak; it's fun to "tweak the tiger's tail." They want attention and get it one way or another. Within a small percentage, distrust escalates into anger and hate. They feel a strong determination to "get them before they get us," or they live by the motto "don't get mad, get even." On rare occasions, suppressed emotions of distrust and resentment may explode into rage.

Some control their feelings by isolating themselves; they do what they have to do and leave when the day is over. Others crave attention and recognition and have found that the only way they can gain it is through extreme negative behavior. A minority deliberately act in ways that are detrimental to the manager or organization. At the low end, they disregard rules and regulations; at the extreme, they sabotage company property or the product or service, and in extreme cases they resort to violence.

Using their aggressiveness, they may attract others in the work group with similar feelings and intentions (which they inflame and exploit). Others engage in criminal activities such as loan sharking, drug pushing and theft of company property. They aggressively harass fellow employees or intimidate supervisors and managers. Employee performance is restricted affecting productivity, quality, costs and morale.

Some of these individuals begin with relatively minor offenses and, over time, increase the seriousness of their actions. They test management's patience and tolerance by pushing beyond all acceptable limits.

Several times each year we read of an employee who has entered the workplace and killed the boss or their fellow employees. Mercifully, these instances are few and far between, but an effective manager has to be aware that this *can* happen and be vigilant.

THE "FOUR HORSEMEN"

Every time there was a problem on the shop floor the same four people were somehow involved. Whether it was a production problem, a shipping problem, or an employee disturbance it could be traced back to these four. They generated a steady stream of complaints.

Brian, the young president, thought of the troublesome quartet as the Four Horsemen of the Apocalypse. Brian had assumed his position a year earlier when his father retired. He had done just about every job in the plant during the years his father groomed him for the presidency.

But he was frustrated by the endless complaints about and by the Four Horsemen and by his inability to correct the situation. The final straw came when the four asked to see him in his office and presented him with their signed union membership application cards.

They threatened to "bring in the union" if their list of demands were not met. (This is unusual because, in most cases, a group such as this would simply have remained underground, signing up other employees without attracting management's attention.) This tactic led us to believe that the foursome weren't genuinely interested in unionizing the plant; it was an ill-conceived power play to make the young president sweat.

In frustration, he called in the authors as consultants.

After interviewing each of the employees, our recommendation was to form an employee association which would represent employee concerns. It would also forestall the entry of a formal union. A relieved Brian, the four instigators and the other employees all agreed to the recommendation.

Problem solved? Not on your life!

Whenever the employee association prepared a list of concerns and recommended solutions, the four would agree and support them. However, as soon as the employee association received the approval of management, the four would reject the approved measures, criticize the employee association, and block progress in any way possible. After a few months of this frustration the employee association committee resigned and advised Brian that no one else would agree to participate. Brian again called in the authors to consult. He was advised to terminate the four and pay the legally required termination pay. Brian was cautioned that the four would likely seek legal counsel and if they went to court, which was likely, they could be awarded additional compensation. This is exactly what happened.

When Brian totaled the applicable costs, he was shocked that they amounted to considerably more than $75,000. But when asked, if he could retrieve this amount, would he take the four back, his response was, "Not on your life, it's the best investment I've ever made."

The Four Horsemen provided a perfect example of how a few employees with extreme behavioral problems deliberately undermine management's efforts and attempt to enlist others to do the same.

FINALLY SAFE – NEVER SORRY

It was an "etched-in-stone" rule, as it is in so many organizations, that safety glasses must be worn in the plant. Steve was a machinist and had been with the company for three years. Although his record of absenteeism and lateness was worse than others, he was careful to limit these infractions. He had a canny feel for what he could and could not get away with. Then for some strange reason he began a game of "catch-me-if-you-can" that involved his safety glasses. He would punch in at the time clock and begin walking into the plant without his glasses. If he saw the supervisor, he would quickly put them on. At other times, he would put them on before entering the plant but then take them off after a few minutes. He would vary his tactics each day.

His supervisor cautioned him that he would have to take disciplinary action if Steve continued. But Steve was enjoying the game too much to quit. So the disciplinary process began, first a verbal cautioning, then a written warning, next a one-day suspension. With each disciplinary step, Steve would insist that the union fight the action with a grievance. He continued his game. To add variety, there were days when he would act normally and follow the rules, then he would begin again.
Other employees quickly became aware of what was happening and enjoyed the distraction. This gave Steve the attention and the status (of sorts) that he craved and it encouraged him to continue.

Steve's supervisor was frantic and frustrated; the union committeeman felt the same. Neither could think of a way to stop the process short of termination, which would require many more hours and days of effort and disruption as the inevitable grievance process wore on. Both asked the company's Labor Relations Manager for help and he scheduled a meeting with Steve, the supervisor, and the union rep.

"Steve," the Labor Relations Manager asked in his laid back style, "your committeeman and supervisor have told me about what's been going on with the safety glasses. Please tell me, do you want to continue working here?"

"Of course I do," Steve replied, "but no one can make me wear safety glasses when I don't want to."

"Let me explain this to you Steve," the Labor Relations Manager responded quietly and calmly. "You are absolutely right. No one can, will or should monitor you to make you wear safety glasses. But you see Steve, it's *a condition of employment* here. If you want this job, you have to wear them at all times in the plant. But if you don't want to be employed here any longer, then of course, you don't have to wear them."

Steve, looked at the committeeman, who nodded in agreement. "No problem, now that I understand that's how things are, I'll wear them."

This game was over. However, it was only a few months until Steve invented a new game to aggravate his supervisor and the company. It took almost a year of disciplinary steps but in the end he was fired. He wouldn't, possibly couldn't, change.

AL'S EXIT

Al's behaviors were much the same as Steve's. A different company, different type of work, different age but a history of deliberate and disruptive actions led to the same result: termination. We only include this brief example because of Al's final words to the owner of the company.

"I don't know why I do it," he said before walking out the door. "I did the same thing at my last job. I just keep doing these things until I go too far. I can't seem to stop myself. Why didn't you fire me sooner? I deserved it."

Al's disruptiveness could have been avoided altogether had those who hired him recognized the pattern of frequent job changes in his employment history and taken the time to do effective reference checks to determine the reasons.

A PRESENT AND THE PRESENTATION

Ross was a loner, sullen and withdrawn. He projected an aura of resentment and suspicion that suggested he carried a "chip on his shoulder." He did his work as required but contributed a sense of uneasiness to the workplace. Normally his supervisor, Art, accepted him as he was and left him alone. Then something came up that was to change Art's perceptions and those of his co-workers.

A well-liked and respected employee was due to retire and an informal presentation was planned for the following month. Art was asked to prepare something to present to the retiree in recognition of his service. It could be humorous or not. Art asked his people for ideas and someone mentioned that Ross had a great natural talent for wood carving. Possibly he could do something unique as a gift. Somewhat unsure as to the reaction he would get, Art told Ross about the idea and how he had heard of Ross's talent. Would he do it? Quietly Ross said he would.

Three weeks later, unobtrusively, he brought in a package wrapped in brown paper and handed it to Art. When he unwrapped it, Art was astounded. It was a work of art, a carving of a fisherman, stream, mountain, clouds, and trees, all done in pine and stained in a light finish. He was speechless. Ross was watching his reaction and relishing it. Art sincerely complimented him in every way that he could think of.

"There's only one thing missing," he said as he turned over the piece and continued. "It needs your signature and date on the back. All great artists sign their work."

With pride, Ross signed and dated the carving using a felt pen.

Art finished by asking if, at the presentation, Ross would hand the carving to the retiree after he said a few words, "It's so well done," Art said, "that you should do it". Ross was so moved that he choked up and couldn't speak. He simply nodded and left.

From that day on, the relationship between these two men was one of mutual respect and understanding. Ross was still a quiet guy, but the tense atmosphere surrounding him had disappeared.

When and why does this type of problem occur?

Disruptive and/or dangerous employees are usually hired with the outlook that makes them so. In some cases their negative beliefs were created by the treatment they received under previous management. Each job change, each new manager, changes in the workplace or in management practices have further reinforced their negativity and therefore justified their negative behaviors. They carry their outlook and behaviors from job to job.

But, the root cause of their distrust of authority often predates their work experience. Some as children or young adults were abused or harassed by people in authority (parents, clergy, teachers, police, physicians, bosses, or others) and have come to believe that those in positions of power don't care about their difficulties, their ideas, or their potential. They feel they are treated as if they are worthless. In some cases, they have difficulty communicating their frustrations clearly and calmly. Therefore, they hold back their feelings, which can eventually explode in rage.

Only recently have researchers learned that others with severe anger problems (in and out of prison) have long had some type of learning disability. This problem has gone undiagnosed, resulting in them being labeled slow learners by teachers and harassed and taunted by fellow students. They received failing grades, dropped out of school, and have ended up in menial jobs, on unemployment or involved in criminal acts, angry and distrustful of all those in authority.

Psychologists are still unsure why some people resort to physical assault, destruction of property or criminal activity.

Only a psychologist, after interviewing the individual, could provide a studied opinion.

The point is that managers must realize what is happening and deal with it firmly, consistently, promptly and with sensitivity. Regardless of the cause, managers must continue to focus their discussions on behavior and performance, offering professional assistance where appropriate.

Fixing it and preventing it in future

The type of individual we are discussing in this chapter may need the "tough love" described in Chapter 11. The situation is most difficult to change because it requires a two-pronged approach:

➤ First, the person who is their direct "boss" has to apply **corrective and progressive discipline** because their behavior warrants it. The individual will deliberately increase the frequency and severity of their negative actions until the person in charge reacts.

➤ Second, even though corrective discipline is being applied and the manager or supervisor is watching for violations, it is important to **observe what is being done well** and if possible identify unique natural talents and accomplishments and to **comment on them positively**.

Some of these individuals respond remarkably well and quickly, when for the first time in their lives, they receive sincere praise and recognition. Unfortunately, a few continue their unacceptable behaviors until they are eventually discharged.

The best form of prevention is to always hire the best people available, those who can and will do what you expect.

In your recruiting, screening and selection process:

➤ Listen carefully for **negative comments** by the applicant. When heard, follow up with questions about previous employers and supervisors to identify opinions and experiences that may have been negative and explore the reasons.

➤ Be particularly alert to an employment record or resumé that indicates **frequent job changes**. They may indicate negative behaviors, unsatisfactory performance, or significant personality clashes.

➤ Unfortunately, when the economy is booming, there may be few suitable candidates with the specific skills required. **Be patient and pursue all avenues other than hiring this type of person.** This may be difficult when the need is great and the time available is short, but a hurried decision may be regretted for years into the future.

CAUTION
Always advise and involve Human Resources personnel when you experience this problem. Keep a detailed record of their offenses because they will usually challenge and deny the facts when discipline or termination is in the offing.
Having the employee initial the record and giving them a copy provides two benefits. First, they cannot deny they were told. Second, it reinforces the seriousness of the situation.

SUPREME CAUTION
Those few individuals who have severe mental disorders requiring professional treatment should not be allowed to return to the workplace until such action is approved by the psychiatrist or psychologist treating them.

Observations

It has taken years for this individual to develop these negative beliefs, don't expect immediate improvement. Dealing with this type of person requires close attention, patience and persistence. It is important to control our own emotions, which could be difficult considering the circumstances. There are times when you may feel angry and frustrated but cannot show it. There will be three great rewards for dealing with this situation effectively. The first is that eventually, in one way or another, it will be resolved. Second, going through this process, difficult and demanding as it is, will be one of your most valuable experiences. Third, others will realize that you will take such action when necessary and will respect you for that.

In some cases, you may penetrate the carefully constructed defenses of this type of individual by identifying some talent, something they do well, some interest you and the employee have in common and something you can talk about. This simple act builds a bridge, a bond between you and the employee and neutralizes the negative emotions the person has bottled up for many years.

The deliberately disruptive are angry (not at us necessarily, but at the world) and they want respect and attention (which they often don't deserve). Watch for actions and accomplishments that justify praise and give it promptly.

In your actions towards them, be particularly firm and fair. If you are not being fair, they recognize it and you unintentionally reinforce their negative beliefs about those in authority.

We have learned that under everyone's hard protective outer shell may be a person who wants to be accepted appreciated and understood.

A trophy is due to every person in a position of authority, who effectively and promptly deals with these types of problems. They should qualify for sainthood on the basis of their courage, initiative, patience, persistence, and performance.

"A great coach will make his players see what they can be rather than what they are."   **– Ara Parseghian**

A Smile Break

Sign in a Rome laundry: "Ladies leave your clothes here and spend the afternoon having a good time."

Another Smile Break

"When leaving work late you will go unnoticed. When leaving work early, you will meet the boss in the parking lot."   **– Lampner's Law**

13

How To Change
Negative
Situations
Into
Positive
Relationships

Imagine we're front-line supervisors in a high volume automotive parts plant. Glancing down an aisle in our department, we see that Ryan, a young new employee is bending over a pallet of material and he isn't wearing his safety glasses. We know that when he was hired two weeks ago, he was given a plant tour, instructed regarding plant rules, and provided with both safety glasses, and safety boots.

Ryan is obviously in violation of company safety rules. The Plant Manager has been absolutely committed to reducing injuries and doing it by eliminating unsafe acts and unsafe conditions.

We have a choice. Since the employee is new we could:

1. Ignore it, believing it won't happen again.
2. Approach him and tell him to "put the glasses on" and give him a stern lecture.

3. Issue a verbal reprimand and make a note of it in his personnel docket.

4. Take a more serious disciplinary action in the form of a written reprimand or a half-day suspension.

What action would you take and why?

This is one of the situations discussed in Unique Development's Leadership 2010 course for Supervisors and Managers. When the facilitators ask for a show of hands, as to whether participants would take disciplinary action, usually 70-80 percent say, "Yes." Another 5-10 percent would ignore the violation and the remaining 15-20 percent usually opts for the stern lecture.

Obviously ignoring the violation is not an option. A stern lecture or a disciplinary action is the most frequently used action. But is it the best?

Review the facts once more. We're dealing with:

➤ A young employee
➤ In a new job
➤ Possibly his first job in a manufacturing plant
➤ Possibly confused about finding the missing item and...
➤ There may be other factors involved (e.g. his safety glasses may not fit properly)

Now if we administer a lecture or discipline, will that create a positive or negative emotion? Will it build or erode the relationship?

Our challenge in management is to constantly develop credibility, trust, respect and a positive relationship – yes, **even in disciplinary situations.**

A more positive step in this case would be to approach the employee and begin by asking, "Are you having a problem?"

Then, if necessary ask, "Is there anything wrong with your safety glasses?" Usually this will trigger the realization of his violation and an explanation. If it doesn't, ask, "Do you remember the safety rule regarding safety glasses?"

In this way we haven't accused the employee of anything, we have gathered useful facts and now better understand the employee's viewpoint.

Now at this point we could administer the lecture and add a warning about the possibility of disciplinary action in the future. Would this approach be seen as caring or callous?

Our challenge is to take this situation and make it a positive experience.

Another approach after asking the questions could be to say, "Ryan you're new here and I'm sure you want to do well so I'm going to share a passion of mine and my greatest fear."

Do you think we have his attention with these words? You bet!

"My great passion," you continue, "is the safety and success of the people in my department, which includes you. My greatest fear is that one of you will have an accident and lose an eye, an arm, a leg, or your life. What a terrible loss that would be. It would affect your life forever. You know I'm afraid it would affect me forever as well."

"But that's not quite my greatest fear. My greatest fear is that I wouldn't know what to say to your wife or your parents. Saying, 'I'm sorry,' couldn't possibly be enough. Saying, 'I told Ryan to be more careful,' wouldn't do it either. Maybe, if I could honestly say, 'I've done everything possible, everything in my power to prevent this happening,' maybe that would help but I know I'd still remember the loss for many years."

"So I need your help, your promise that you will do everything possible to work safely, do it consciously every day and keep a lookout for others. Can I count on you?"

Such an approach builds respect and a relationship not only with that person but with others who eventually learn about it. **We build a positive reputation by what we say and how we say it.**

DEMOTE OR DEVELOP – WHAT ABOUT BOB?

Gary had a performance problem. It disappointed him. It frustrated him. It was all because of Jeff. Five months before he had selected Jeff from the hourly employee ranks and promoted him to supervisor. Thinking back, he knew why: Jeff was bright, reliable, a hard-worker, cooperative, and likeable. In addition, Jeff knew the operations in several departments. Definitely a winner, Gary had thought. That was then, this was now.

Jeff's department was meeting the shipping schedules, quality was great and his department was efficient. However, soon after his promotion Jeff had begun displaying negative behaviors. He was increasingly critical of his people. Often he resorted to put-downs and disparaging remarks. Employees claimed he was acting "high and mighty," felt he was "better than the people he had worked with." They resented his methods. They became less cooperative and the number of grievances began to increase.

Gary had met with Jeff several times to coach and mentor him. They had discussed the need to improve Jeff's people skills. Jeff always agreed he would do better but nothing changed. When asked why, Jeff's answer was, "I don't see what I'm doing wrong and don't know how to do it differently."

Gary felt that he had done all he could do. He was frustrated because he still liked Jeff and felt that Jeff had great abilities and qualities. Demoting Jeff back to the hourly ranks would please the employees but it would ruin Jeff's career. Plus, life would be difficult for him back on the shop floor. In desperation, Gary searched the area for a leadership course that would be appropriate. It had to be practical; it had to be light on theories, and heavy on how-to-do-skills. Finally, it had to contain assignments which would require on-the-job application. Once he'd found the right course he called Jeff into his office. He was tempted to order Jeff to take the course but that could have caused possible opposition, resentment, and refusal. Thinking about it, he had a hunch that, if his opinion of Jeff was correct,

Jeff would welcome the opportunity. If he was wrong about Jeff, Jeff would turn it down.

In the conversation, he avoided being negative in any way. He didn't point out the deteriorating situation in Jeff's department or the employee complaints.

"Jeff," he said, "when I chose you for promotion it was because of your abilities, experience, personality, and willingness to do whatever needed to be done. I want you to know that, even though there have been some challenges, I still believe I made the right decision. That doesn't get us off the hook. We haven't, as yet, found a way to smooth out this rocky situation and get you on your way to success."

"Now I've found a course that I expect will help. It's one evening a week over ten weeks. It's practical and requires learning new skills and applying them. Are you willing to devote ten of your evenings to this effort?"

"You bet I am," Jeff answered without hesitation. "When do I start?"

"Yes," Gary thought. "I picked the right man. He will succeed."

After the fourth week of the course Gary was beginning to hear comments such as, "Jeff is changing." It was time to talk about the course, so he met with Jeff.

"How is the course going?" he asked. "What have they got you doing?"

"It's going great," Jeff responded. "They've got us doing two things. First, we had to select a project to improve some aspect of performance in our department, involve the employees and be prepared to present the results at the last session of the course. By the way our "bosses" are invited to attend that session. Second, we have an assignment to 'get to know our people.'"

He handed Gary a sheet of paper. "This is a form they gave us to track what we've learned," he said. "It has a column for the employee's name, what they do well, their interests outside of work, and what they are proudest of having achieved.

You know, it's opened my eyes. These are good people and they have many of the same interests as I do. Now we have something to talk about other than work."

The employees were saying the same about Jeff. For the first time he had a positive relationship with his people.

So a performance problem properly handled was win-win for everyone, for Jeff, Gary, and the employees. Oh yes, we musn't forget, it was a win for the company as well.

WHAT'S WANTED VS. WHAT'S BEST

An opportunity sometimes creates a challenge as difficult as a performance problem. Often, a problem is an opportunity in disguise.

The rumor mill was saying that a management position was becoming available. Jerry was a supervisor with six years experience in the department and felt he had the necessary qualifications. Waiting for the right opening, he approached Peter, his manager, and made his interest known. Peter in turn promised to pass the information up to his Vice President, Kevin, which he did.

For Peter and Kevin this was a "hot potato." What made it such a hot issue was that, although Jerry had been a supervisor for six years, his poor relations with people in the workplace made his performance barely acceptable. Other candidates were more qualified and one of these would likely be selected for the position.

Kevin changed the direction and tenor of the discussion when he asked Peter a question.

"Peter," he said, "I know from our discussions over the years that Jerry's basic weakness is his people skills, tell me two things: what are his strengths and what type of position would best suit those strengths? Let's not try to answer these here and now. Look back over past performance reviews, think of his assignments over the years, and consider past projects. Think of one or two that got him excited and enthused. In the meantime tell Jerry that we've discussed his request and will talk to him in a few days."

Fortunately, the company was a large financial institution with six regional offices, hundreds of branches, and a large corporate head office. The size of the business increased the scope of what was available and the number of options.

At their next meeting the two managers listed Jerry's strengths: numerical and analytical skills, experience in several functional areas and a personal interest in real estate and investments.

Then Peter had a revelation.

"You know," he said, "while we realize that Jerry lacks the supervisory people skills, he is outstanding in customer-related skills. He enjoys dealing with customers, their problems, and their goals."

Thinking about potential positions for Jerry, they identified three. Now they were ready for their discussion with Jerry.

Kevin led the conversation. He began by telling Jerry frankly that the upcoming managerial position would be going to a more qualified candidate. Then he said, "Jerry your interest in this position triggered some creative thinking by Peter and myself. Realizing you were interested in a career change, we sat down and listed your strengths and abilities. I'll read the list to you."

When he finished he asked, "Does this describe you fairly?"

Jerry just nodded because he was too emotional to speak.

"What about the comment that you seem to enjoy working with customers more than working with employees?" Kevin asked. "Is that correct?"

Again, Jerry nodded in agreement.

"Then let me share an idea," Kevin continued, "a possibility, that Peter and I came up with. There are openings from time to time for Personal Trust Officers. These people meet with and advise clients on managing their estates, investments, property, and their personal affairs generally. It's a serious responsibility and not everyone is suited but we think it could be perfect for you. While the salary is about the same as what you are earning now, the job satisfaction could be greater and the employee hassles eliminated. How do you feel about this possibility?" .

"It all sounds perfect," Jerry cautiously responded, "but this is very sudden. Can I think about it for a couple of days?"

"Certainly," Kevin said. "But as you do, please realize this won't happen immediately, it may take a few months. We should consider it your career goal and work towards it. In the meantime, discuss it with your wife, keep it confidential and we will, over time, make it happen."

After five months, a position came open, Jerry got it. He was successful and enjoyed it. Peter was able to move a more suitable person into Jerry's position. Everyone was a winner.

Observations

The above examples and similar stories throughout this book illustrate the powerful results achieved by developing positive solutions to employee problems.

Organizational success will continue to be evaluated on top-line revenue growth, bottom-line profit increases, and market penetration gains. However, too seldom recognized are the managers, executives, and first-line supervisors who find creative win-win solutions to everyday problems do it with care and passion and thereby contribute to the organization's success.

14   Now You Know ...
GO FOR IT!

Most employees want to do what's expected of them and want to do it well. Of course, at the other extreme are a few who do as little as they can "get away with" and an even smaller number who deserve to be discharged and virtually dare the manager to do it.

As we consider the twelve reasons that employees don't do what we expect, we realize that most of them naturally fall into five groups:

1. Those who are **prevented or hampered** by a lack of information, knowledge, and resources or who are restricted in their performance by others. They *could* do, *want* to do and *would* do what you expect *if they had the knowledge and information* they require and if their manager would provide it.

2. Those who are **not naturally suited** to the requirements of their job because of abilities, interests, personality characteristics or values. They cannot easily and effectively do what the job entails. *They could likely perform well in some other position.*

3. Those who are **demotivated** by the negative culture and circumstances. They *could* do, *want* to do and *would* do what is expected *if management took action to correct the negative aspects of the workplace.*

4. Those who are hampered by **personal problems or illness**. They *can't* do, but some *want* to do and some *would* do *if they could get the professional help they need to turn their lives around.*

All of the above situations require some action on the part of management to remove the barriers and hindrances that restrict their performance.

Where do we start and what do we need to do?

When asked these questions, the wise old author on the mountain top said: "Start where you are, move in the direction you need to go, do what you need to do, ask for help when you need help and keep moving until you get to where you need to go."

Isn't this advice irritating? That's because it's simple and it's true.

Look once more at the Getting Started section. There it was mentioned that most problems are due to the reasons covered in the early chapters, and fewer problems are due to those explored in the final chapters.

Begin by being aware of what is and is not being done, of what is and is not happening and of what the results are. Then recognize, praise, and support what is being done well. Next begin to remove obstacles to improved performance for those who want to and will be effective. Your people will realize that you are taking needed action and will begin to assist and respond. Once you get the ball rolling use the 12 reasons as a checklist for improvements. Always begin first with what is possible for you to do – the things you can do relatively easily, quickly and at minimum cost. Then tackle the more difficult issues. Work tirelessly for continuous improvement. Finally, always share the glory.

The key to success, the most vital element for each of us, the thing we need to do first and always, is to check our personal attitudes, beliefs and perceptions.

Then choose to be a Great Manager rather than a Grim Manager. The differences are as follows:

GREAT Managers	GRIM Managers
Attitudes	
- Positive and supportive - Believes most employees want to do well, care about the company and welcome responsibility - Others have many ideas	- Negative and critical - Believes most employees are lazy, don't care about the company and avoid responsibility - Others have few ideas
Emotions	
- Trusting - Respect others	- Suspicious - Little respect for others
Actions	
- Coach, counsel, and compliment - Relationship and task-focused - Friendly/open - Goals/encouragement - Engaged/involved - Focus on prevention	- Criticize, coerce, and complain - Totally task-focused - Aloof/closed - Rules/enforcement - Reserved/absent - Focus on correction

The two types differ as well in regard to their personal development, priorities, and commitment:

GREAT Managers	GRIM Managers
- Know their people therefore gain respect, trust, and cooperation.	- Disregard their people therefore are distrusted and generate confrontation.
- Pursue problems, solve and prevent recurrence in future. Involve the employees and gain support.	- Avoid problems. Not concerned about future. Ignore employees and experience opposition.
- Develop a network of trusted peers and advisors so gain advice and cooperation when needed.	- Self-reliant, too busy, not worth the effort, don't need or value the advice of others.
- Know the budgeting/ approvals process and therefore are usually better able to obtain the resources they need.	- Don't know the process. Feel it's too complicated, too time consuming, and not worthwhile finding out.
- Understand the total process and how their department relates to internal suppliers and internal and external customers from receipt of order to final shipment.	- Unconcerned about the overall process. Only concerned about their own departmental activities.

GREAT Managers	GRIM Managers
- Develop their knowledge of human resources policies, procedures, and past practices. Therefore are confident in dealing with employee problems on an appropriate and progressive basis.	- Because of their uncertainty, often avoid or ignore correction until the problem escalates out of control. Then they overreact.
- Are aware of and manage appropriately outstanding performers, satisfactory performers, and problem performers.	- Tend to ignore outstanding and good performers. Overly focus on problem employees. Therefore lose the support of their best people.
- Believe in continuous learning and therefore search out training opportunities. Will pay for courses themselves if necessary.	- Believe they "know it all' and avoid training opportunities. Say, "It's a waste of time" but often fear possible failure.
- Believe training, coaching, and mentoring employees leads to improved performance, generates trust and cooperation and minimizes errors. Understand that trial and error is the most expensive, frustrating, and dangerous approach.	- Believe that employees should learn themselves, through trial and error. "No one showed me," is often their comment. Make excuses such as "We don't have the time or the budget, we can't do it now for umpteen reasons."

Observations

Grim managers, by avoidance, lack of knowledge, fear of failure, or negligence or ego, often create the very problems they wish they could avoid.

Grim managers can't be bothered to do what's recommended, their excuses range from "we shouldn't have to" and "we can't afford it" to "we're too busy" and on and on. Life for them is arduous, a constant hassle, filled with arguments, resistance and pain.

Great managers make the time and take the time to do all of the things that prevent problems and build employee support, respect, and trust. Therefore, they make it all look easy and simple.

"The only real security that a person can have in this world is a reserve of knowledge, experience, and ability."   - Henry Ford, Industrialist

---

Index

Acknowledgements

This book is the sum total of all we have researched and experienced. Its content comes not only from ourselves but from the many clients who have shared their struggles and successes. We are grateful for the opportunity to be a part of their lives and challenges. We have not attempted to cite all of the materials, references and resources that we have accessed in the preparation of this work. That simply would have been overwhelming.

To begin, we thank Rob Way, former editor of *London Business Magazine* who accepted our first articles for publication and suggested we put a book on our "To Do" list.

Our content readers Jeri Anderson, Doug Dolman, Jeff Keenor and Dick Lawrence who were invaluable, first because of their diversity of experience and knowledge and, second, because of their dedication and perseverance. Their detailed comments and suggestions were always well considered and appropriate.

The comments and expertise of Natalie Allen, Professor of Psychology, University of Western Ontario provided answers when needed. Similarly, our thanks to Dr. David Krueger for permission to use excerpts from his book *Emotional Business*.

Thanks are also due to Tamelynda Lux for the many hours she spent inputting and proofreading the material and, to Marilyn Broad for proofreading. Andrew Borkowski, thank you for your professional editing and for adding words and phrases to make the content more understandable and readable. To Gord Breckenreid of Rapport Creative – our appreciation for the front and back cover design, and to Christine Mach of Double Q Printing who formatted the manuscript.

Finally we acknowledge the many writers who have written on similar topics and influenced our thoughts and perceptions over many years.

About the Authors

Irwin Schinkel completed his business education at McMaster University, then joined the world's largest automaker and served in two major divisions—a high volume, highly diversified automotive parts division and a heavy transportation equipment division that exported to 29 countries. He held management positions in Sales/Marketing, Strategic Planning and Human Resources. Electing early retirement, he established Unique Development Corporation in 1987. Irwin's focus has been on providing medium and large family businesses with strategies and skills to cope with change and on helping them seize opportunities for growth. He is a passionate believer that people at all levels in an organization need practical solutions, applicable skills and achievable strategies.

Greg Schinkel graduated from the Richard Ivey School of Business, having studied management systems at Kettering University in Flint, Michigan. After a variety of positions in the automotive industry he joined Unique Development in 1990 and acquired the company in 1992. As president of the firm he has grown the capabilities and the revenues of the company. In the past decade he has facilitated hundreds of workshops in team building, leadership development and value-based sales techniques. He is a high energy speaker and a Director of the Canadian Association of Professional Speakers. Greg is also a National Director with the Canadian Association of Family Enterprise. Greg's commitment is twofold, working with medium-sized family businesses and multi-plant and multi-national organizations. Specifically, he believes in linking training and consulting and using both to maximize the synergism of management and employees at all levels. In this way it is possible to achieve breakthrough, sustainable improvement and best-ever performance levels.

Talk To Us: We Listen – and Respond!

We sincerely hope that you have enjoyed this book and have experienced the expected benefits. Your comments, suggestions, or personal experiences would be much appreciated. Kindly indicate your permission to use them in future editions of this book or in other books being written. If you prefer that they not be shared we will respect that wish.

Contact us if you would like ideas on how to use this book as a training resource within your organization. These possibilities range from keynote speeches to overview seminars, skill development workshops, application strategies or consulting assistance in identifying, prioritizing and implementing improvement initiatives.

Resources mentioned in the book such as the assessment process for hiring selection and promotion decisions (which we referred to as "Chuck's Treasure") are available for your use. Similarly we can assist you with organizational culture/climate surveys to identify areas where opportunities for improvement are greatest.

Our skilled associates have significant expertise in a wide variety of organizational areas such as:

➤ **Leadership Development**, which includes executive coaching and mentoring.

➤ **Organizational Synergism**, which links executive goals and strategies with middle management, supervisors and frontline employees to ensure focus, implementation and actual achievement, then ensures the sustainability of those gains and continuous improvement.

➤ **Sales Force Effectiveness**, including all of the elements that impact the success of the sales organization from hiring and training to rewarding and motivating. We design these elements specifically for your challenges, products/services and people.

Unique Development Corporation has trained more than 10,000 people in over 700 companies. It is equally adept at developing leadership skills at the executive level and at the shop floor level and linking the two to achieve increasingly challenging goals.

Whatever your needs and planned initiatives we would be excited and enthused at an opportunity to assist you in achieving them. Contact Greg Schinkel at:

Unique Development Corporation
45 Meg Drive
London, Ontario, Canada N6E 2V2
Tel: 1-800-622-6437 / Fax: 519-685-9043
E-mail: gschinkel@uniquedevelopment.com
Website: www.uniquedevelopment.com

Maximize Your Success

Subscribe to our *Unique People* e-newsletter – It's Free!

Receive practical and insightful ideas about leadership, sales, and operational effectiveness in a concise format. Use the order form on the last page to start your free subscription.

Order the *Employees Not Doing What You Expect Practical Application Guide*

Achieve the maximum impact from applying the ideas and methods from this book by purchasing the companion guide. The **Practical Application Guide** includes:

➤ Application binder
➤ Additional content and information
➤ Worksheets
➤ Samples
➤ Audio CD

Use the **Practical Application Guide** to:

➤ Identify your specific expectations of others.
➤ Assess the capability of your people to meet those expectations.
➤ Identify and eliminate obstacles to performance.
➤ Coach employees to even higher levels of performance.
➤ Confront and correct employees who continue to not meet your expectations.

Order your copy by using the order form on the last page.

Congratulations to all of our readers who are committed to learning, growing, and being positive leaders and great managers. You are a powerful influence on the careers and lives of so many. We wish you every continuing success.

- Greg and Irwin Schinkel

QUICK ORDER FORM
Four easy ways for you to order.

1. Fax orders: (519) 685-9043 using this form.

2. Telephone orders: Call (800) 622-6437 toll free, or
(519) 685-2116. PLEASE HAVE YOUR CREDIT CARD READY.

3. Email orders: orders@uniquedevelopment.com

4. Postal orders: Unique Development Corporation,
45 Meg Drive, London, Ontario, Canada N6E 2V2

❑ Please send me _____ additional copies of *"Employees Not Doing What You Expect"* @ $29.95 CDN or $24.95 U.S + S&H.

❑ I'm interested in purchasing more than 5 copies of the book. Please send information regarding volume discounts.

❑ Please send me _____ copies of the *"Employees Not Doing What You Expect"* Practical Application Guide @ $175.00 CDN or $150.00 US + S&H.

❑ Begin my FREE subscription to the Unique People e-newsletter

❑ Provide additional information about:

_____

Name: _____

Address: _____

City: _____ State/Prov: _____ Zip/PCode: _____

Telephone: _____

Email: _____

Sales Tax: Please add 7% GST for products shipped to Canadian address.

Shipping by Air: Canada/USA $7.00 for first book or disk and $2.00 for each additional product.

International: $9.00 for first book or disk and $5.00 for each additional product.

PAYMENT: ❑ VISA ❑ MASTERCARD ❑ CHEQUE/MONEY ORDER

Card Number: _____

Name on Card: _____ Exp. Date _____

Signature: _____